ISBN-13: 978-0982370858

Books by Jonathan Pritchard

[Learn] **Like A Mind Reader**
Perfect **Recall**

[Think]
Like A Mind Reader

Improve your business, strengthen your relationships, and solve your problems.

Contents

This Book is
Dedicated to:

Ashley

Thank you for showing me what
dedication really looks like.

Preface

When we're born, the universe is nothing but a swirl of light, sound, and sensation. There's nothing but direct experience. Pretty quickly we figure out that there's an "out there" and an "in here." We are separate and distinct from the crazy light show we're witnessing. For example, our shoe comes off, but our foot doesn't. We learn language that we can use to ask for things, let others know how we feel, and share what we're thinking.

Thinking! What a strange experience. It's like we're a pure ego living in our skull who's been tasked with driving this big meat puppet we call "our body." We might have random impulses to hit our sibling. What's more, we might even do it! Our parents tell us, "Now, Jonathan. Good little boys don't hit their brothers. They don't even think about hitting their brothers." And we learn there are thoughts we aren't allowed to think. We retreat further into our minds, and choose to identify with only the parts we like. We call this our persona. We continue to live our lives, further refining our persona based on feedback from others about what works and what doesn't work, to get us what we want.

The problem, however, is that at each stage of development, we get farther and farther away from our experience. We get deeper and deeper into our heads. This can be an intensely lonely experience, but there's a way out. That's why I'm writing this book. I'm sharing the thoughts, experiences, and techniques I've learned and applied over a lifetime to live full of excitement, adventure, and deep connection with the people I love. If you feel like your life is lacking, you're in the right place. If you need help in your business, you're in the right place. Because really, business is simply human relationships plus dollars, right?! The better you know yourself, the better you can know your customers, and the better you can serve everyone in that equation.

My goal for having you read this book is to turn your thinking inside out. I want you to see the world in ways you never thought possible. I want you to see opportunity at every turn. That's what it means to think like a mind reader.

Welcome to my thoughts.

Introduction

Over the past ten years I've made a living as a professional mentalist. That means I get paid to convince people I can read minds. I've done a USO tour where I entertained United States troops stationed overseas; I've been on national television; I've performed on Vegas mainstages, partied hard, and barely lived to tell the story. Basically every single checkbox you could have as a performer I've checked off once or twice, all while doing it the way I wanted to. I spend my time where I want, doing what I want, and with the people I want.

I call that success.

This book is written in response to hundreds of conversations I've had over the years with people who stick around after shows, once the autograph line dies down. They say things like, "Man! You are living the dream! You travel the world, get paid good money, have fun at work, and you don't have to work in cubicle hell. I can't even imagine living a life that like."

After hearing different versions of the same thing enough times, it hit me:

They literally can't imagine living a life like mine.

Their imagination has slowly been drained from them. Worn away by standardized testing, misguided caution from their family and friends, and their own doubts about what they're capable of.

The result, however, is millions of people living without the slightest inkling of how to create a life they're actually excited to live. To them, Monday is a day to dread at the office, not another day to have adventures.

Mondays don't suck. Your job sucks.

Eventually I started getting more jazzed to talk with people after my show than I was to do the show, because I wasn't just making them forget how miserable their lives are for an hour. Instead, I was turning their thinking inside out, opening their eyes to what's possible in life, and sharing the mental secrets I've discovered that will help them live an adventure most people can never dream of.

And now I want to help you.

Inside this book you'll find the exact same strategies I've used in my own life to get creative, make more money, have incredible relationships, and solve my problems.

Now, don't make the mistake of thinking I've always

had it easy. I haven't. The ideas I'm sharing have been battle-tested through divorce, being broke and homeless, and dealing with intense self-doubt, fear, and depression.

This isn't pie-in-the-sky positive thinking. This is cold hard truth about how the mind works, and how to make it work for you to get what you want out of life.

See you on the other side.

Chapter 1: Mental Efficiency

If there's nothing else you take from this book, let it be this: Organizing your mind is the single most important thing you can do. Organization is one of the most powerful forces in your life. It is what helps you rail against entropy, chaos, that overwhelming sense of doom that creeps up on you when you accidentally leave the TV off while you're eating dinner.

Just like it is with any power, though, it doesn't happen for free. It takes massive effort and energy. And just like it is with any skill, it gets easier the better you get at it.

We tend to fight organizing our mind because it reminds us of "the system" called "school" that removed our creativity so slowly and deftly, we didn't even notice it happening. Our days seemed to be set up specifically to dehumanize us, our choices reduced to obeying bells that rang at exactly the same time every day.

Some people find that comforting; but it made me feel like I was in prison, not a place known for fostering a healthy sense of self-worth.

So I can understand why you might not want to spend

time thinking about organizing your mind. You might think it's not worth the effort, and that's where you'd be mistaken.

Your whole life will benefit from the power of organized thinking. The mind is the starting point for everything. Nothing can be done without it.

Think about a group of people trying to move a boulder blocking the road. If each person pushes whenever they want in whatever direction they want, they're never going to get it to budge. If, however, they coordinate their efforts and push in the same direction at the same time, they're much more likely to move it out of their way and continue on their path.

The same goes for your mind.

If all your thoughts are scattered, you will be less effective at moving the metaphorical boulders in your life. The bad news is, you've created them, and put them in your own way. The good news is, you've created them, so there's nothing stopping you from removing them with the power of organized thought.

You have to be your own efficiency expert. Organizations and companies will spend millions of dollars to have people comb through their business to find places where they can be more efficient. That's because they know how expensive wasted time really is.

You can always get more money, but you can never get more time.

Think about it. Organization is control. You have control of your mind. Maybe not right now you don't, but that's what this book is helping you with!

Businesses have systems for everything. Everything. Without them, there is no repeatable process. Organized solutions are the fastest, easiest, most cost-effective way to solve problems. And like these companies, you want to get the most return out of the least amount of effort.

The first ingredient in effective thinking is preparation. It helps you anticipate future problems, obstacles, challenges, and surprises. This is where anxiety actually becomes helpful. If you weren't anxious about what could go wrong, you'd never plan for it, and then you'd waste even more time when broadsided by a simple problem. Anticipating and preparing for possible outcomes will save you time in the long run.

Take a note from companies that invest heavily in doing things as efficiently as possible. Plan and prepare for the future, and tolerate no redundancy in your life. Wasteful thinking is to be eliminated with no hesitation.

Truth: you can do something about the direction your

life is headed. Before you can move forward, you have to accept this as the universal truth it is. There is only one person in control of your thoughts, and it's you.

Until you come to grips with this, you will never make progress. Until you stop blaming others for the choices you make, you will never make progress. Until you take responsibility for your actions, you will never make progress.

BUT. The next challenge is to do something with what you learn.

The fact you're still reading gives me hope that you understand how high the stakes are; you're betting the rest of your life on the choices you're making right now. You're interested in what else you can find inside these thoughts I'm sharing with you, and that's the first hurdle to learning; being interested.

Sadly, the world is almost entirely full of talkers, not doers. They talk about this mystical land of "someday." They "might someday" do this. They "might someday" do that. How many people do you know who have that dream they're always talking about, but you know they haven't taken one step towards it?

Sadly, they're the people most in need of help, and they're the least likely to look for it. They seem to have an excuse behind every opportunity they let pass by. They have "snowflake syndrome" where they tell themselves, "That solution won't work because of my completely unique situation that's never existed for anyone else since the dawn of time. That thing that's already worked for millions of people won't work for me. It's not because I'm obstinate and scared."

Or maybe they say, "I'd give anything for what you have!" Well, what if I told you that the "cost" is the time to read this book and apply what you learn? "Oh, I'm much too busy thinking about dealing with these bullshit problems that I've created as a distraction to actually do anything about it. Sorry!"

You can see how frustrating it can be to know that the people who would benefit the most will never find this book. That's why I'm counting on you to apply what you learn, and live as an example. Lead with action. Live with integrity. Serve as someone others can look to for an idea of what it means to have a good life.

"Whether you think you can or whether you think you can't, you're right." **~Henry Ford**

Thoughts Aren't Real -- But They Make Your Reality

Good thinking simply means being in control of your thoughts and finding the best solutions to your problems as quickly as possible. When you're too busy being stressed out, distracted, or confused then there's no amount of thinking that will get you where you want to go. The quality of your solutions is only as good as the quality of thinking that creates them. When most of your thinking is centered around problem-solving (which it is), this is massively important.

You may not choose what happens to you, but you can choose what to do about it. This is the essence of problem-solving. You have an idea (what you think the problem "means"), and then you go about either proving or disproving that idea by testing your hypothesis. This is what shapes your decision-making.

Who Do You Believe? Me, or You?

When you tell yourself what something means, you tend to believe yourself, too. Magicians have known this for thousands of years. Shamans in prehistory probably understood this, too.

Consider these two possibilities. First, a magician shuffles cards while saying, "This is a perfectly ordinary deck of cards in every way. No trick cards here. Only cards like you'd find at home in your junk drawer that you yourself may own." Or, second, a magician shuffles a deck of cards, hands them to a person in the front row, and asks them to "shuffle the cards as much as you like."

Which one seems more suspicious? The first, of course!

"Why would he call attention to the fact that they might be trick cards if they're actually normal? Why not just act like they're normal cards?"

Why indeed?

While the first example is more obviously suspicious, it's actually the second example that's more likely to involve a trick deck. Since the magician casually hands the deck to a person in the audience and asks them to shuffle, your subconscious says, "Well, he handed the cards out which he wouldn't do if there were some trick to them, so they have to be normal." He's allowing you to trick yourself. You believe the lie you tell yourself more than any truth he could speak.

This process of letting people fool themselves works like a charm, and is at the heart of understanding that you are in charge of interpreting what your experiences mean. Remember that in the second case above, you're telling yourself that the experience of handing out the cards means they must be completely normal.

This plays out in everyday life, too. When you're constantly asking yourself, "Why am I such a loser and have horrible things happen to me? Why can't I ever find the time for what I want to do? Why can't I just lose that weight?" your mind will search for, and then find, a reason to support the hypothesis that you're a loser. Problem solved! And, since it's something you're telling yourself, you believe it more than any truth someone else could tell you.

Further, it makes no difference how near or far your idea is from reality. Your mind will tell you it's real so it doesn't have to think too hard. I run into this all the time doing tricks at parties.

I've spent a lifetime getting pretty good at sleight of hand. I can make impossible magic happen with an absolutely normal deck of cards. Every once in awhile someone will say, "Oh, if I had that trick deck, I could do that too." They're absolutely certain the magic is merely the result of a trick deck, and not decades of practice. Their completely inaccurate solution feels exactly the same as if they had actually figured out the real method. Relevancy to reality makes no difference. Their mind tells them it's real, so they believe it is.

That's why most of your fears feel so certain. Your mind makes them so. The cool thing is, you can do exactly the same thing with confidence-boosting thoughts and empowering beliefs about what you can achieve.

That's why it's absolutely essential to get an accurate perception of how things actually are, consider what it means without negative assumptions, and then choose answers that empower you to take positive action. See things as they are, not how you want them to be.

I know what you're thinking. You think you already see things without bias. While that might be the case, there's a very real biological quirk in our eyes to illustrate the point that you probably don't.

In the area where our optic nerves connect to our retina, there are no photoreceptors. You literally have a blind spot you never notice because your mind "fills in" what it thinks should be there. Here's how to see for yourself.

On a blank piece of paper, draw a quarter-inch square, then about four inches to the right draw a quarter-inch circle. Make sure to color them all the way in. Hold the paper at arm's length and close your left eye. Look at the square with your right eye and slowly bring the paper closer to your face. When the paper is about six inches away from your face, the circle will disappear. That's because it's entering your blind spot, and your brain fills in with its best guess based on what else it's seeing. Since that's mostly white paper, that's what your brain tells you to see. So you see it.

Same goes with your thoughts, beliefs, and decisions. You have certain psychological blind spots about what other people's' motivations are, why they do what they do, what they think about you, and so on. You can't know all of those things for certain. Unless you're a mind reader. Which I am. So take my word for it.

Focused Concentration
vs. Daydreaming

If you're thinking about doing anything, you need to get organized. No matter what the goal is, making it happen will require consistent focus to reach it. The bigger the goal, the more demanding the effort will be to make it a reality.

Anything else is daydreaming.

Don't get me wrong; daydreaming can be useful. Can be. But only so far as it helps you figure out what you truly want.

What commonly happens is people get the same feel-good sensations from thinking about doing something (daydreaming) as they would from actually doing the thing. They start enjoying the imaginary thing more than the real thing, and it makes sense; that takes no effort! Why try when all you have to do is think?

This is why so many people dream of writing, painting, or any other kind of creative endeavor. The work in your mind is always better than anything you could actually do in the real world, which is incredibly frustrating. When you're only frustrated with your work it's difficult to continue working at it, but it's the only way to improve the quality of your work. Do more of it! Don't think about it, do it!

This is also why I don't tell people to rely on public accountability.

Motivation gurus will advise you to tell everyone you're going to do something so they can hold you accountable. This winds up backfiring. Everyone chimes in on your wall with "OMG! You get it! You're amazing!" and, again, you get all the feel-good chemicals going and you haven't even done a single thing to get you closer to your goal.

Instead, commit to it yourself. Maybe tell one person who you know will be supportive as your accountability-buddy. Then put in the hard work. Your results will speak for themselves, and then you get the luxury of having accomplished something amazing and having everyone tell you you're incredible. It's a positive reinforcement sandwich!

When it comes to figuring out how to take that first step, that's where the power of your daydreaming comes to play. Remember, "nothing is good or bad, but thinking makes it so." Put your efforts into the best use of your time, as time is your most precious resource. You can always get more money (sell plasma!), but you can never get more time once yours runs out. Focus on organizing what you have so you can put it to its most efficient ends.

The mind is boundless. It continues inward forever. There's no limit to how much you can learn or what you can do when you finally grasp the most important secret: make up your mind to improve, and you will!

Consider this the short introduction to what you'll find in the rest of the book. Basically, a mind that is well-organized leaves no room for fear, uncertainty, second guessing, choice paralysis, or whatever has been holding you back lately.

An organized mind will help you identify and act upon the proper options. It will help you solve your problems quickly, efficiently, and permanently. It will help you trade self-defeating habits with good ones on all fronts.

An organized mind will help you live a happier, more successful, less stressful life. There are countless areas where we could talk about how the right mindset will help you, but I've chosen to limit this book to what I consider to be the most essential.

Once you understand the impact the ideas in this book can have on those areas, you'll quickly understand how to apply good thinking to all other areas of your life.

Chapter 2: Get Interested -- Be Successful

A gift (or curse depending on how you look at it) of being a mentalist is being able to see the future. Not just any future; yours, in fact. As I sit in a coffee shop in Chicago writing the words you're reading, I'm allowing my mind to travel forward through time to this exact moment, and I bring you a message.

You are going to die alone.

In fact, you're already alone. You've always been alone. From the moment you were born until the instant you die, you're alone.

You've felt this. You know it's true. There's an ever-present sense that you're the only person you can be sure is real. Even in the most crowded room, you're an island to yourself.

There's this sense that even if you were born as someone else, you'd still have that same feeling of "I"ness that is forever trapped inside whatever mind is around to bear witness to it.

You know everyone else is in their own existential

nightmare, too, right? We have social conventions like asking people how they're feeling when we meet. If they answered honestly they'd grab you by the shirt and scream, "I'm terrified of dying alone, but that's what's going to happen and I can't stop it!" But they don't. Everyone says, "I'm good, you?"

You shouldn't worry too much about what people think of you. I say this as an authority on what people think about, and I can tell you they're not spending much time on you. Nobody cares. They don't. They're too busy quietly freaking out about their own mortality and the host of problems they've created for themselves as a distraction from the only truth in life.

You will die alone.

That's why your problems don't matter to other people. Your problems belong to you, nobody else. And the same goes in the other direction, too. Nobody's problems are quite so worthy of your attention as your own problems, right?

That's it. That's the message. Feels like a bummer, right? At least now you know I'm not here peddling feel-good platitudes to people so I can make millions of dollars off the gullible.

I don't say all this to get you more depressed than you were already. In fact, when you realize the full impact of what it means for you, you'll discover it's quite liberating.

Even though you're all alone, so is everybody else. That means there's a way of easing the crushing weight of solitude. You have to go beyond what your tiny ego is telling you. It's the ego that keeps you trapped in the prison of isolation. It tells you it's the most important thing in the world, and as you know from Chapter 1, you tend to believe what you tell yourself. The longer you believe there's an "I" rattling around in that brain of yours, the more difficult it will be to dismantle that illusion.

How are you supposed to move beyond this complete and all-consuming self-absorption?

It's quite simple really: be interested in other people.

It's 100 percent that simple. Notice, however, I'm saying "simple" and not "easy." If you've already had a lifetime's practice of being wrapped up in your own self-made universe of problems, worries, wants, and desires, it can be phenomenally difficult to even pretend to care about someone else.

But you can do it!

Like any new skill, it will be difficult at first. You'll have to find some way to trick yourself into being interested in others. But sooner than you might expect you'll find yourself getting more and more interested in other people.

There's a good exercise that will get you started on the right path, and I want to tell you about a fun time I had in college to help you understand it.

I think it was my sophomore year when I signed up to be a beta tester for what would become the wildly successful computer game "World of Warcraft." It's played online with thousands of other people from all over the globe. You pick your character and then run off to explore a virtual world that's incredibly rich. You can team up with your real-life friends, or with people you've never met before, to be your "adventure buddies." Together you can defeat bad guys that are too powerful to fight on your own. While most of the characters you meet in the game are avatars for real human beings, there are certain characters that aren't; think shopkeepers, bad guys, etc. These are called, appropriately enough, Non-Player Characters, or "NPCs" for short. They follow relatively simple decision trees, and draw from a limited conversation resource. They're not designed to be featured characters on your adventure; they're usually part of the background.

Sounds familiar, right? You're the hero of your own real-life adventure. Most of the people you meet are essentially NPCs to you. You share limited conversation. You stick to safe conversation topics like the weather. You treat them like NPCs. Very few people you meet will ever break through to the level of "adventure buddy."

The trick, then, is to remind yourself they're not NPCs. They are experiencing an "I" just like you are. They're living their own adventure that's just as rich and meaningful as yours. There's a word in German for this idea: sonder.

This is the first step in relieving the unbearable loneliness of being.

Once you truly see everyone you meet as another "I" you'll start to care about them. If you care about them, you'll feel compelled to do something about it. This is why so many people throughout history have (correctly) identified that the fastest way to help yourself is to help someone else. Another way of putting it is to be the friend you wish you had. Suddenly, you'll have more friends than you can count.

Note: I'm not advocating prioritizing others over your own well-being; that is not a feasible long-term solution. There's a reason flight attendants tell you to put your mask on first. You're no good to anyone dead.

It's also important to point out that you can't lie your

way into this. It absolutely can't be a quid pro quo "I did this, so you do that" kind of deal. You can't have the motive of getting something from people. That's manipulation, and people can feel that. That approach would only serve to isolate you even further. You might get away with it for awhile, but you can't fool yourself, and that guilt will manifest itself somehow.

Neither the mercenary approach (this for that), nor the martyr approach (but I gave you everything!) will help you. Only by cultivating an honest appreciation for others, and being interested in their journey, will do it.

Bridge the Gap

You've taken a moment to stop navel-gazing at your own problems, so now turn your attention to what you imagine other people are concerned with.

Take a cue from every Tarot card reader who ever set up shop. It doesn't matter what culture or country you're from, there are only a handful of topics people worry about. The specifics might be different, but the topics always center around relationships, money, or health. That's it. Help others find solutions to those problems, and you'll get everything you've ever wanted.

A business is "be the friend you'd want to have" with dollars involved. If you're having a tough time in your business, it's quite likely you're focused on what your customer could do for you, and not the other way around. If your employees aren't performing like they should, you're probably focused on how their sales numbers are reflecting on you, not on showing them how to improve so they can get what they want out of the job. I can't tell you how many sales meetings I've been to where the manager tries to get the crowd fired up by saying, "Come on everybody! I need your best out there today! If we cross that mark I get a new car!" Who cares?! I have medical bills from my spouse, and here you are talking about a new car? I don't think so.

As it is in personal relationships, having an honest interest in others and what they want is the fastest way to get others interested in you.

People will recognize you're not listening only to find your spot to jump in. You'll actually be giving your full attention. This will make the other person feel important. You're treating them like they're important because they are important!

Every single person you'll ever meet has lived a life you will never live. This means they know things about life that you don't. This opportunity may be the one and only time you have to learn what that thing is. Skip the polite chitchat. Cut right to the core. Lay their experience bare. If you do this with honesty and genuine interest, you'll be amazed what people will share with you.

This can be done by simply avoiding the script everyone's reading from. Instead of asking them, "So, what do you do?" ask, instead, "What's something you're excited about?" Ask them, "What's something you're looking forward to" It's that easy. If nothing else, they'll love you for not being boring! Then, no matter what they answer, actually listen to what they have to say. This is easy since you have no idea what they're about to tell you. That makes it more interesting for you, too!

The more interested you are, the more you'll want to listen. The more you listen, the more interesting people get. It's a positive feedback loop of connection.

"But People Are Awful"

I get it. There's a lot to not like about people. They're selfish, mean, gossipy, and generally unpleasant to be around. Plus, if you dislike someone, I know it's difficult to be interested in them.

The thing is, though, you don't see people as they are. You see them as you are.

There's a saying I love that goes something like this: "Meet a jerk in the morning, you met a jerk. Meet nothing but jerks all day, you're the jerk." Don't be surprised if you can rattle off a list of fifty people you don't like if you're at the top of all their lists, too! Those who hate are the most hated.

You might be wondering why I've spent so much time talking about this stuff. I'm trying to get across how everything in your life is affected by the way you think about things. Everything you've done or ever will do is the result of setting your mind to it. Focus that power on the negative, and that's what you'll get; negativity.

What you choose to be interested in absolutely is a choice. You can choose to be interested in things that will improve your life, and the more of those beneficial things you focus on, the better your life will be. Nobody else will do it for you. All the teachers in the world can show you the door, but you're the one who has to walk through it. The doorway, in this case, is realizing and taking responsibility for how your interests shape the outcome of your life. Take charge of it, and you take charge of your life.

If you think I'm beating a dead horse, you're not wrong, yet we're not done with it either. Don't gloss over this point. Other people might like to coast through life without admitting they care about something, but you're not that person anymore. That kind of apathy and lack of enthusiasm for life won't serve you where you want to go.

Long story short, when you genuinely get interested in other people, you help everyone involved in that equation. Them, you, and everyone else you connect with from that point forward. As a matter of fact, this is the reason I'm writing this book! I'm trying to have these conversations with you, the reader, even though we may never be in the same place at the same time; yet you're still able to share my thoughts.

A big mistake you might be tempted to make at this point is to nod your head along with everything you've read so far, and then take it no farther. That won't do you any good. For this stuff to actually improve your life, you have to put it into practice. Do something with it! If you read this book and nothing good comes from it, I'm not to blame. You are. Don't get upset at the results you don't get from the work you didn't do. This stuff works. It's worked for me, it's worked for my mentors, and it's worked for every single successful person throughout history. The amount it will work for you is directly related to how hard you work it for yourself.

The problem is that you think you have enough time to worry about this stuff later. You don't. Your house is on fire, and you need to do something about it right now. Not later. There is no later; only this moment.

If you're still just agreeing with me in an abstract sense without ever dreaming of applying anything you learn, you should put the book down now. Nothing's worse than lukewarm enthusiasm. I'd either want you riled up with me, or against me; just as long as you're fired up about something!

Chapter 3: Get Enthusiastic

"There is a real magic in enthusiasm. It spells the difference between mediocrity and accomplishment."
~Norman Vincent Peale

Think about the most incredible human accomplishments throughout history. Think any of them were done by someone who didn't have enthusiasm? Absolutely not. Sure, you might be able to do things at a high level without enthusiasm, but no truly great achievement is possible without it. This is why sales is often said to be simply the transfer of enthusiasm. A salesperson who lacks enthusiasm for his product will never be truly great. If he doesn't care about what he's selling, then why should his client? (Hint: They won't!)

In order to learn anything new, try something different, or reach past your comfort zone, you'll absolutely need to develop enthusiasm. It makes every single thing easier to do. It's the secret ingredient that can make the difference when all other things are equal. The person with more enthusiasm will always win. It can even make up for a lack of knowledge, resources, or experience.

Who would you rather date? Someone who, on paper, is a perfect match but isn't enthusiastic about the idea, or someone who you might not consider at first, but shows considerable enthusiasm for spending time with you? (Ideally you won't have to make a choice like this in your life, but you get the point.)

So how do you lose your enthusiasm? Tell yourself you "have to." Obligation is the archenemy of enthusiasm. You know what, though? You don't have to do anything. Every single thing you do is because you choose to do it. When you remember it's a choice you're making, you rediscover the opportunity to appreciate why you're making that choice instead of another. Once you realize it's something you want to do instead of an obligation you're fulfilling, then you'll find space for enthusiasm.

Instead of thinking, "This is something I have to do," tell yourself, "This is something I'm choosing to do, and I'm someone who enjoys it!" This approach will help you feel more enthusiastic for three reasons. First, it's our old friend self-trust (you believe what you tell yourself). Second is the power of commitment. You want to be someone who is "true to their word" so you'll tend to follow through on your stated intentions. This is a powerful psychological technique called "consistency," where people tend to behave in alignment with how they are described (by themselves and by others).

I use this all the time in my show when choosing

spectators. I will say, "I need the help of a volunteer who likes to have a great time and likes to laugh!" Then, no matter what we do on stage, that volunteer will interpret the experience as fun and enjoyable, even if what we do together might be potentially embarrassing.

This is how performers can get away with some pretty outlandish stuff on stage that would never fly in the real world, through the combination of those three powerful psychological forces: self-trust, commitment, and consistency. By agreeing to join me on stage, they are telling themselves and everyone around them that they like to have a good time and laugh. This is a public commitment. If, while onstage, they don't appear to be having a good time, that would be inconsistent with their stated personality of being fun-loving, which in turn leads to cognitive dissonance. In order to minimize that possibility, their mind will interpret everything that happens on stage as "enjoyable and fun."

Leverage the power of consistency, and commitment to cultivate enthusiasm in your life, for things you may not appreciate right now. Tell yourself you enjoy something, and magically you open the possibility of actually enjoying it! That's why we went into so much detail talking about being interested in others. If you lack that interest to begin with, the only way to start is to get enthusiastic about what you can learn from everyone you meet.

The most dynamic, engaging, and interesting people I've ever met are themselves, enthusiastic and interested in life! Just like only boring people are bored, only interested people are interesting. That's why I can't allow tepid interest in my life, and neither can you.

Cultivate that kind of enthusiasm in your day-to-day life, and watch how your experiences transform. Instead of being just another NPC in someone else's droll life, you'll suddenly be the single spark of sunlight in an otherwise unremarkable day. You'll have that fire for life, that spark of vitality that is contagious. You'll walk into a room and everyone will be drawn to you as if by some unseen magnetic force; that's the power of enthusiasm and interest for life.

What's In It For Me?

Maybe you don't want to light up a room. Maybe you don't want to get recognition in your industry. Maybe you don't want to have tons of money.

But you do have to want something. There has to be some incentive to go through all this work. The incentive is your "why." Why are you doing all this? Without a why, nothing is worth doing (let alone doing well).

Too many people confuse their "what" for their "why." They can tell you what they want to accomplish, but not why they want to do it. Without the why, however, no what is going to be good enough. To distract themselves from this glaring gap in their life, they tell themselves the comforting lie, "I'm doing the best I can."

I don't think so.

There's always room for improvement. There's always something you can learn. The instant you think you're at the top is the exact second you can mark the start of your downfall. The only time you're not learning is when you're dead. Otherwise you can always improve.

If you genuinely believe you're doing the best you can, you're going to stagnate. You're not going to improve. You're going to behave in alignment with the personal affirmation that this effort is the best you can do. To believe that's your best is to set an artificially low cap on your progress and potential.

Don't sabotage your ability to do better. Set your goals beyond what you think is possible. This will force you to become a person who is capable of achieving that goal, even if you're not that person right now. That kind of progress is exciting. You'll get fired up, and enthusiastic about how to get more results like that. You'll become deeply interested in success, and you'll be a better person for it.

Unbearable Gumption

"Gumption" is an old-school word like "moxie" that means spirited initiative and resourcefulness. It's having the audacity to start something, and the wiles to make it happen. Basically it's turbo-charged confidence.

What would your life be like if you had the confidence that no matter what came your way, you'd be able to handle it? The cool thing is, you already can. Once that confidence is in your marrow, you'll feel like the most powerful person on the planet!

You'll also be the most powerful person on the planet.

Think about any news story about a citizen hero. They almost always say exactly the same thing, "I was just doing what anyone would do in the same situation." You think, "There's no way I'd be able to do it!" It's amazing, however, what you can do when you have to.

You probably already do this. It's called "procrastination." You wait until the last minute as a way to build up psychological pressure that finally gets to be more uncomfortable than the pain of not doing the project, so you're now backed into a corner that you have to get out of. So you stay up until the wee hours of the morning, and finish the project with just moments to spare.

This is a strategy that works. Maybe not the best approach, but it works. I'm not saying you should intentionally put things off until the last minute as a way to get things done. What I am saying, however, is recognize the same enthusiasm for problem solving, incentive development, and initiative that you're in control of in that dynamic. Then put that to use in your way to create that same feeling of being cornered, without actually being in danger of running out of time and failing.

Once you see that you can take control of this dynamic in various contexts, you'll build confidence that you can do amazing things in a timely manner with energy to spare. Most of what you've gotten done in your life so far is the result of resisting external circumstances until you're forced to change, like pressure building in a champagne bottle before the cork pops.

Use that process of cultivating enthusiasm, interest, and incentive to your advantage. You'll solve your problems more quickly and efficiently without wasting time focusing on the problem itself. Once you've established the habit of problem solving (instead of problem worrying), you'll believe you can manage any kind of challenge that comes your way. And, because of that belief, you'll be right!

Autosuggestion

Belief is the precursor of all accomplishment. Remember the Henry Ford quote, "Whether you think you can or whether you think you can't, you're right." This is a form of autosuggestion, or self-hypnosis.

One of my best friends on the planet, CJ Johnson, is a gifted hypnotist. (Matter of fact, he's amazing at plenty of things, but for now I'm going to focus on the hypnosis angle.) He explained hypnosis to me as "creating social dynamics where people are rewarded for following my suggestions, and not rewarded for not following my suggestions."

Basically, CJ is fantastic at creating situations where people want to follow his suggestions. Through this simple (but not easy) approach, CJ can get people to believe, through and through, that they are something they're not. Or that a shoe is a puppy. Or that their arm is too heavy to lift off their lap.

There's almost no end to what CJ can get a hypnotized subject to do (as long as it's not against the subject's personal value system; he can't create a "Manchurian Candidate" situation, for example). The common thread, however, is the belief. Once he can convince someone to accept an idea (like that their arm is too heavy), the subject can't help but to behave in alignment with that belief (so they won't be able to lift their arm). Nothing changes about the physical makeup of their arm; it's all in their mind. But that doesn't stop the experience from feeling 100 percent real, because their beliefs dictate what they're capable of experiencing and the mind makes it real.

We do this to ourselves every day, all day long. We tell ourselves, "Oh I could never do X," and we believe it. Since we believe what we tell ourselves, our minds make that limitation real, so it feels 100 percent real that we lack that ability. We are so easily influenced by our own opinions, and the opinions of others. Every single suggestion can be made real by your mind. If you're not careful to guard against it, you'll allow yourself to be swayed by your friends, family, and even strangers whose job it is to affect your thinking. (They're called advertisers.)

"Are you going to let your nose itch like that forever? How long has it been itchy like that? Why don't you go ahead and scratch it? It would feel so good!"

If you're like most people, you probably just felt the tiniest little tickle in your nose. It's just like catching a yawn; we're social creatures, and being in tune with how other people are feeling is an evolutionary benefit that allows you to be mindful of appropriate behaviors, and how those behaviors would affect your chances of staying with the group instead of being ostracized. But this influence can work against you, especially when you're berating yourself.

The effects of this form of self-hypnosis isn't limited to the mind. It's very real in the physical realm, too. It's called the "ideomotor response," and I saw it all the time when I worked with professional skeptic James Randi at his foundation, handling applications for his Million Dollar Paranormal Challenge. The challenge was very simple. You think you have a supernatural ability like reading minds, seeing the future, or moving things with your mind? Tell us what you can do, with what accuracy, and in what situations. Shouldn't take more than two paragraphs, really. Once we understand what you're claiming to do we'll design a double blind pass/fail test to evaluate it. Pass the test, and get a million dollars.

Of the thousands who applied, not a single person got past the first round of testing.

Most folks couldn't even say what it is they could do. Instead, we regularly got 80 handwritten pages talking about "when the moon is in the third house of Venus and the retrograde of this demon is at its peak" with writing in the margins, coffee stains, and so on. But, despite all the duds, we did get a bunch of applicants who could follow the process. Most of those people were dowsers; they claimed to be able to find water, oil, gold, or whatever you wanted with a forked stick, a pendulum, or whatever their dad had taught them to use. Every single one said exactly the same thing. "I know you probably hear this a lot, but I'm actually the real deal. Everybody else says they can do this, but they're doing it wrong. My way, though, is the way that works, and I'm going to win that money. Hope you're ready to be proved wrong!"

Every. Single. Dowser.

Dowsing works on a simple principle known as the ideomotor response. It's what makes Ouija boards work. The movement of the planchet (the little thing everyone puts their hands on that moves around the board) is the result of subconscious muscle movements that are perceived as coming from the outside. It really feels like some outside force is moving it; that's what makes it such a compelling experience. The user isn't consciously aware they're the one making the movement happen.

Dowsers all have their own prefered methods, but they're all based on creating a contraption that is very sensitive to the slightest movement which will amplify small motion into larger motion. The most common are forked sticks, a pendulum (a simple weight on a string), or bent coat hangers that cross. The idea is that the Dowser holds their contraption over a sample of whatever they're looking for to "tune" their device to the right "frequency." Once dialed in, they'll walk around until the pendulum goes crazy, which indicates the location of the gold, oil, or whatever.

Turns out, this is pretty easy to test. Here's what you do.

If the Dowser says he (it's always a he, by the way), can find water. Perfect. Get ten cups, line them up with a foot or two between each, and put water in one of them. Have him calibrate his device. "Oh yeah, it's workin' good today!" he says as the pendulum goes crazy over the water. It stays dead still over the empty cups. Then, as he watches, you move the water to a new position before putting a five-gallon bucket over each cup. Have him test his pendulum again. You'll see his pendulum go crazy over the cup with water in it. Not a twitch over the empty cups. This is to prove the covers hiding the water will not interfere with his powers. Just like dirt won't interfere with his ability to find water out in the field, or gold coins under the sand on a beach.

Now the fun starts.

He's "proven" he can detect water under the buckets which present no interference to his abilities.

Now the test can begin for real.

He's asked to step outside the testing area so the

placement of the water can be totally randomized. Once the water is placed under a bucket, everyone who knows where the water is leaves the area, too. Now, he's allowed back into the room. Nobody present knows where the water is, and this is an important part; it precludes anyone unwittingly betraying the information through subconscious gestures or behaviors. (This is the first part of the double blind process.)

He's allowed to take as much time as he likes to find the water. Once he's sure he's found it ("It's definitely under bucket 3!"), his choice is recorded, he leaves the room, the water is randomly placed again, and the process is repeated. He comes in, chooses a position, his choice is recorded, and he leaves.

The reason you don't tell him whether or not he's right is so to not influence his confidence if he gets them wrong (this is the second part of the double blind process). Because he will get them wrong, on average nine out of ten times.

When the possibility of personal knowledge influencing behavior is removed, Dowsers do exactly as well as if you'd rolled dice. No better than chance. They'd get it right exactly as often as if you'd asked a baby to point at one of the buckets ten times.

This indicates that the pendulum's movement over

water during the "calibration" is the result of the Dowser's own knowledge influencing the outcome, and not the result of some unseen force that, if real, would totally revolutionize physics as we know it.

If you want to experience it for yourself, try this experiment.

Get a foot-long piece of string and tie a small pebble to one end. Now get a deck of cards and put several cards face up on the table. Holding the string by the very end, let the pebble hang just above the cards. Now, see very clearly in your mind that the stone will swing in a straight line (back and forth) over black cards, and in a circle over red cards.

Give the pebble a little swing, and hold it over one card at a time. Give it long enough, and you'll see the pebble do what I've said it will. Back and forth over black cards, and in a circle over red cards. Don't try to make it swing, but also don't keep it from swinging.

Before long you'll have the knack to make it happen every time without fail. That is, until you decide to turn the cards face down, shuffle them up, and then see what the pendulum does. You'll find you're right about half the time. Exactly the same odds as if you'd flipped a coin. That's because it's your own mind making your muscles move, and the length of the pendulum multiplies that tiny movement into a bigger swing that feels like it's moving on its own.

Neat trick and all, but what does it mean? It proves that what you're enthusiastic about, what you believe in, and what you're expecting to happen will help it happen! You can use these principles in your own life, consciously, to achieve things you're telling yourself are impossible right now. Don't let these processes run on autopilot. Take control of them, and make them work for you!

We're all affected by our personal beliefs in regards to what we can accomplish. It's like we have some sort of internal "achievement thermostat" that defines the upper and lower levels of what we can do. We don't do too little. We don't do too much. We stay within our comfortable zone.

We have our own ideas of who we are, what we want to do, and what we can do, that we don't like challenging. It's uncomfortable.

Stop being afraid of what you're capable of! Stop being afraid of "what could happen if it goes wrong?" Set your sights higher. Demand more of yourself. Believe you can, and you'll be amazed at how much you can do. You'll retrain your subconscious to develop an enthusiastic approach to problem-solving, and you'll discover that mistakes will only serve to work harder to prove your limitations wrong. If you're someone who never tries anything for fear of failure, you'll certainly fail. Because the only thing worse than trying and failing is never trying in the first place. The only way to learn is to learn from your mistakes, and make more interesting mistakes in the future. As long as you're making better mistakes, you're getting better.

Believe, in your core, that you can do something, and your mind will have no choice but to help you make it happen. This will feel strange at first, especially if you're someone who has spent a lifetime focused on "what can go wrong" instead of "what can go right." Don't move away from what you don't want.

Move towards what you do want. I've met thousands of people who can go on forever telling me what they don't like, but can't think of one thing they do like. Be the single person in a thousand who has the gumption to 1) know what you want, and 2) believe you can have it.

When combining those two principles, it will feel like the universe is conspiring to help you succeed. It's not some outside force acting on your life. It's really your own beliefs acting in your life. You're the power. You are the force of the universe made real.

Act like it.

Virtuous Selfishness

Why would you go through all this trouble to get your mind right? Should you do it for your spouse? Your family? Your business? Your customers? Strangers on the street?

Yourself, that's who. You.

Without selfishness, there would be no incentive to improve. If you base your motivation on someone else's approval, you'll forever be the slave to someone else's whim; your foundations will be built on their opinion of you.

But, when you give enough of a damn about your own well-being to do something about it, that's the good kind of selfishness. This is putting your oxygen mask on first, as I've mentioned before.

Success requires you to be audacious in the sense that you have to be selfish enough to think you deserve the best out of life. Not to impress someone else. Not to harm someone else. Have enough gumption to demand the best, and you're on the right track.

This enthusiasm for your own well-being and happiness is infectious, too. Human beings are fantastically empathetic; we're really good at picking up on how others are feeling. As I said earlier, it's a positive evolutionary tactic to encourage group cohesion. People who are completely oblivious to those around them wind up becoming isolated. So if you're good at picking up how others are feeling, the flip side is true, too; others are good at picking up how you're feeling! If you're always broadcasting negativity and doubt, that's what everyone around you is going to pick up. And since we're influenced by our environment, you're responsible for negatively influencing the people around you when you're focused on failure.

If you have the audacity to be happy, you're going to transfer that enthusiasm for life to everyone you meet. Remember how I said business is the transference of enthusiasm to the client from the salesperson? This is why. A great salesperson gets deeply interested in his client, not in how much his commission will be. The money part takes care of itself once you figure out the human part.

I tend to use business examples because, want it or not, we're all salespeople at heart. You might not be in the business of sales, but you're constantly selling your thoughts, opinions, wants, etc. to those around you. Ever tried to get your sweetie to go to the restaurant you want? That's sales. Doesn't matter what your job is, your entire life is sales.

That's why I say that being interested in other people

is the secret to success. If you fill your mind with the desire to understand others, you won't leave room for self-doubt, sabotage, or other destructive and useless mental habits.

Spend too much time wallowing in your own problems, and you'll realize you're the only person at your pity party. If you don't have time for others, they won't have time for you.

The only thing holding you back from everything you could ever want out of life is the imaginary chain you believe is real.

It's like an elephant growing up with a chain around its leg. When it's fully grown, the chain can be taken off, but the elephant will always behave like it's still there.

Same goes for you.

As long as you think there's something holding you back, it might as well be a chain forged from the strongest metals. This is the essence of self-delusion. The only way to free yourself is to get interested in what's beyond the well-worn territory you've kept to so far. The answer is be interested in people and, by extension, success.

Chapter 4: Think Effectively

Having thoughts isn't the same as thinking effectively. That's like someone saying they're a social media guru because they know how to post something to Facebook. The problem is nailing down what, exactly, constitutes "thinking."

A quick trip to dictionary.com will show you there are 28 definitions of "think." The ones we're mostly concerned with tend to be associated with making decisions, considering consequences, remembering past experiences, evaluating options, or anticipating future events.

Thinking is the single thread that unifies all of those. If you think about it long enough you'll recognize they can be easily sorted into three temporal states. Thinking in the "now" is problem-solving. Thinking in the "past" is remembering. Thinking in the "future" is anticipation.

Each mode is incredibly important to living the best life possible. I heard somewhere the idea that if you're depressed, you're thinking in the past. If you're anxious, you're thinking in the future. If you're happy, you're living in the present.

The quality of our lives is directly related to the quality

of our thinking about the big stuff, and the little stuff in the past, present, and future. If you don't remember anything, you lack an essential tool to effective problem-solving. Imagine how much time you lose if you have to start from scratch every day. Imagine how much time you would lose if you could never anticipate anything, and only deal with what's right in front of you. What kind of skyscraper could you build without plans? Any time you're thinking about the results you want, you're involved with future-state matters.

Have you ever stopped to think about why we even have thoughts in the first place? What's the use of all these mental creations that aren't even real?

Need fulfilment. That's it. Thinking is nature's way of helping us answer the question, "How am I going to get this need met?" Thoughts are the possible answers to that most basic problem. Consider this: if you have everything you could ever want, how motivated are you going to be to find answers? Not very, you already have them! But if you're missing a need, you can bet your bottom dollar you're not going to be happy.

The only constant in life is change, so what works today may very well not work tomorrow. That's why having a mind that can think effectively is one of the most powerful tools for happiness. You constantly have to be reevaluating your strategies for meeting your needs, and the more efficiently you can do that, the happier you're going to be.

Too many people take this for granted. They think because they have thoughts, they assume they're good quality thoughts. But, since they're not good at effective thinking, they don't realize how bad their thoughts actually are. This is the heart of the Dunning-Kruger Effect; a cognitive bias where people with low ability are convinced they're really good at something because they lack the understanding of just how bad they are. Conversely, people who are really good at something understand how much they don't know, so they rate themselves as being much less capable than they actually are. The problem with the quality of thinking is if you never consider how bad you are at thinking, it'll never dawn on you that you could do something about it.

It's a vicious self-reinforcing cycle of incompetence. Welcome to the way out.

Art vs. Science

Science can tell us a lot about neurons firing and what else happens when we think, but like any other skill it's an art to put it into practice. And the word "practice" tells us a major secret to success: it has to be done consistently to stay sharp. Think about the concert pianist who only plays once a year. How good are they going to be compared to someone who plays for several hours every day. There's no comparison!

People often get bogged down at this point thinking about talent versus skill. That's when I love to remind folks of the Kevin Durant quote, "Hard work beats talent when talent doesn't work hard." It doesn't really matter how good you are naturally compared to what you can do with practice, right effort, and time.

The problem is, most of our thinking is definitely not ideal. We run on autopilot too much. We rely on our assumptions too much. We slip into old habits because it's easier. There are plenty of reasons for why most of our thinking is ineffective, and even the simple act of having those reasons on your radar is a big step forward in limiting their negative impact. We'll be covering some of the big ones later in this chapter, and more later in other chapters, too.

One of the biggest is our ever-quickening lifestyles. Never before in the history of human beings have we had so many time-saving conveniences, so why do we all feel like there's never enough time? Well, one part of the puzzle is that lots of folks work in jobs that are pure drudgery for an entire third of their day.

Think data entry, repetitive factory positions, or some sort of mindless task for 480 minutes of every day. 28,800 seconds of every day, five days a week. That's a lot of life to slog through without the demand of having to think.

Sure, if you were going to graph the level of thinking required, there would be a spike at the beginning where the person learns how to do their job, but very quickly the line of "amount of mental effort required" would drop way too close to zero for my liking.

So they spend 33 percent of their day enduring the crushing effort of sucking it up and behaving like an adult. Then they think to themselves, "You know what? I've earned it. I'm deserve to chill out when I get home." Then they sit in front of the television or computer screen and sacrifice their mental reserves on the altar of Netflix.

Want to hear something terrifying? Here's what Netflix CEO, Reed Hastings, said in April 2017: "You know, think about it, when you watch a show from Netflix and you get addicted to it, you stay up late at night. You really — we're competing with sleep, on the margin. And so, it's a very large pool of time."

The number one competitor of Netflix isn't Amazon, HBO, or YouTube. It's sleep. It's that "very large pool of time." Sleep is another third of your life you don't have available to you. No wonder staying up to binge another season of your favorite show is so tempting!

So how do we combat this? Do we campaign against Netflix? The internet? Movies? Videogames? Absolutely not. Everyone has their vices, and it's important to remember what Abraham Lincoln said: "It has been my experience that folks who have no vices have very few virtues." I know I have mine! Instead of outlawing mindless entertainment, it's important to recognize the importance of dedicating time to think.

If you put even the smallest effort towards improving the quality of your thinking, you'll be amazed at the results. It's just as important as going to the gym or eating right. You're human, the combination of mental and physical; and both require sustained effort to stay in shape. And just like how it is with the physical realm, it's easier to maintain than it is to repair.

Socratic Intelligence
"I know that I know nothing." ~**Socrates**

Thinking by itself isn't enough to be effective. Effective thinking is the result of two other things coming together: knowledge and organization. The quality of "information in" rarely leads to better quality "information out." The reason you're having problems with something is that you don't have enough knowledge about the situation. If you have absolutely no context for understanding a situation, it makes sense that you'll lack a solid place from which to start planning. This results in disaster. Since thoughts are what direct your actions, it's no wonder your efforts haven't been getting you what you want.

How do you go about getting more knowledge? You have to put in the time and effort to find it! The good news is there are only a couple ways you can get more knowledge about your problems.

One way is through experience. That's why I love the Mark Twain quote, "Good judgement is the result of experience and experience the result of bad judgement." Another way is through absorbing societal knowledge. What would your friends do? What do you see your neighbors doing? What do you see characters on TV doing in your situation? These are all places we (unknowingly) look to for answers. The last place to look for knowledge is to talk with people who are doing what we want to be doing. Next best, if you can't talk directly with them, is to read anything they've written (like this book!). Or, nowadays, it's pretty easy to find hours of interviews on YouTube you can have playing in the background while you work.

But there's a trap you have to look out for when you're looking for knowledge, and that's not to focus solely on things that reinforce what you already believe. I can't tell you how many times someone has asked me for advice after a talk, and wind up arguing with me! What they're really looking for is their idea in my voice; they're not ready for something that contradicts their pre-established beliefs. That's why I love this quote from Otto von Bismarck: "Only a fool learns from his own mistakes. The wise man learns from the mistakes of others." If they could learn from the lessons I'm sharing with them that I learned through my experience (because I'm a fool!), they'd be geniuses. So, make sure when you experience resistance to what someone is telling you, it's not just your own limited perspective trying to keep you uninformed.

As we've covered already, just because you talk with a lot of people, read articles, and have thoughts, doesn't automatically mean you're gaining valuable knowledge and information. Nor are you absorbing everything you are exposed to. Our senses aren't designed to take in information. Rather, they're designed to filter out most of what we see, hear, think, and experience. There's so much going on all the time that we'd be overwhelmed if we were aware of it all. We only pay attention to what we are interested in. That's why it's so important to be interested in what we don't understand. Other people. Experiences that are different from ours. Listen more, and talk less. Also, be sure when you're learning, you're paying attention with your mind, and not just your eyes. How many times have you been reading a book only to realize five pages later that you have no memory of what you've read? Your mind has wandered off thinking about that vacation you went on when you were twelve years old.

Your eyes saw the page, but your mind was a million miles away.

It's because you weren't interested in what you were reading. To be truly great at something, you have to know it inside and out. That's the mark of an amazing salesperson; they know everything there is to know about what they're selling. Not only that, they know exactly what objections people are going to have to it. And even further, the great salesperson has five answers to every objection to each of those objections! That's the genius of Napoleon, the military and political leader through the French Revolution. He was known for being able to think on his feet and respond quickly to surprising situations. His genius wasn't on the battlefield, however. It was being so interested in how things might play out that he was able to consider every eventuality and possible outcome. He had his answers long before he needed them, and remained flexible to how they were applied in real time. He was so thoroughly invested in success that he devoted his whole being to thinking effectively about his situation.

All of his pre-planning and battlefield ingenuity would have been wasted if the quality of information he received from his spies and scouts was wrong. Garbage in, garbage out. His success was only as good as the information he had to work with!

That's why if you want to excel in anything, you

have to learn as much about it as possible, and never stop learning. There's always something new you can uncover. That's why this section is under "Socratic Intelligence." The instant you think you know everything, you stop growing. The way to keep an open mind is to tell yourself you don't know anything, and that there's still so much yet to learn.

This is the essence of the four stages of competence. At first you're unaware of how little you know about something. This is "Unconscious Incompetence." You literally don't know what you don't know. After some experience you gain some context to understand how much you don't know. This is "Conscious Incompetence." If you stick with it long enough, however, you'll be able to execute the skill, but it will require your full attention. This is "Conscious Competence." Then, once the skill is "in your bones" you can do it without even thinking about it. It's second nature at this point. You can even do something else while you do it. This is "Unconscious Competence."

The problem with living in the unconscious competence realm is forgetting how difficult it was to get there. We like to forget the time and effort it required, so when we try to teach someone else how to do something, we can get frustrated with how slow their progress is, or why "they just don't get it?!" But, this is the process of acquiring any new skill. You cannot bypass these four stages. If you're trying to teach someone else something you know already, be patient with them. If you're trying to teach yourself something you don't know, be patient with yourself. You'll get it eventually with enough knowledge and experience.

But knowledge isn't the only part of the equation. You could have all the knowledge in the world, but if it lacks organization it's not going to do you much good. It's like a library with the world's best "how to" books, but there are no titles on the covers, and similar topics aren't kept together. You'd have to spend so much time looking for the relevant information that it's almost not worth it.

Organization is absolutely essential for effective thinking. This has been my biggest challenge over time. My mind likes to go in eleven different directions at the same time, and each thought could go in eleven more directions, and soon I'm on a completely different topic that has nothing to do with what I wanted to figure out. This is the essence of monkey mind. Organization, however, is the antidote. Organized thinking is the application of knowledge and experience to a specific goal or outcome. Without it, nothing gets done, and it's the reason why daydreaming is not the same as effective thinking.

Organized thinking requires concentration, and if you lack experience doing it, it's going to be difficult.

The reason you're not good at it already is you haven't spent the time required to get good at it! You don't know what you don't know about concentration. The good news is you won't have to live in a monastery in the mountains for years meditating to get better at it. Try this simple exercise instead.

Next time you want to find a solution, or think about a problem, don't just think about it. Write it all down.

When we leave our thoughts in our minds it's easy to get stuck in a loop. No matter how hard we try not to, we wind up coming back around to where we started. That's where writing helps. When you write your thoughts down, it's right there on the page. And I do mean page. Don't just type things out, it's not the same. Go old school. Use paper. Use ink, not pencil. There's no going back! Handwrite your thoughts, and you're involving your whole body in expressing your ideas. One leads to another, and since you only write in one direction, it helps you avoid coming back to the beginning.

Don't just think your thoughts; do them! Writing is a simple but effective way to put thoughts into action.

PreThoughts

We like to believe thoughts come before emotions, but that's what your brain wants you to believe. Of course your ego is going to say it's the most important part of the equation; that's its job. Our emotions, however, predate thoughts on an evolutionary and personal scale. Babies laugh and cry years before they're able to verbalize. Thinking and language are abstract reasoning capabilities whereas emotions are a deep-seated part of our being.

It's useful, then, to think of emotions as barometers for how well our needs are being met, and not as an excuse for our actions. Too many people use "I was angry" as an excuse for poor decisions. Think with your mind, not your emotions! Our emotions aren't good or bad, they just are. It's what you tell yourself your emotions mean that really matters. When you allow yourself to react to your emotions without taking time to think about what they're trying to tell you, you are opening yourself up to prejudice.

When your thoughts about what your emotions mean (I'm upset she didn't remember my birthday which means she doesn't care about me anymore!) are accepted without question, you're allowing yourself to prejudge the situation you're experiencing. This is exactly what prejudice means, and it has much deeper implications.

What we tell ourselves what our experiences mean then let that dictate what we believe about the world. Our beliefs affect what we expect to see in future experiences, so our minds only search for evidence that supports our idea of how the world works. You then cherry-pick only the experiences that support your beliefs, which only reinforces your confidence in how accurate your belief system is. The problem is, these beliefs about what things mean are picked up in early childhood. If you haven't gone through the process of really, truly digging into what you believe, you're making choices on what's essentially the logic of a five-year-old. How comfortable would you be to let a kindergartener make big life choices for you? If you haven't done the deep exercise of working through your mental and emotional structures, that's what you're doing every day, all day long!

Your emotional logic tells you that you already know what things mean, and that you should do something about it, not sit there and think. But that's where prejudice comes in. You'd be surprised how often things aren't how you've judged them to be if you give yourself the opportunity to see them as they truly are.

It pays to learn this lesson. Literally.

My first job after graduating college was working with Theatre Magic, which was the magic shop at Universal Studios theme park in Orlando, Florida. We sold trick decks of cards, gags, novelties, and souvenirs. My job was to demonstrate several magic tricks in a fifteen-minute show, and then tell everyone watching where they could buy every single thing I did. If someone bought the whole package, it would easily be a couple hundred dollars. For someone on commission, that was the holy grail!

As much as I hate to admit it, I allowed myself to be swayed by prejudice. I assumed the people who looked rich would buy more stuff. I'd pay more attention to the people who were in fancy clothes. I'd engage in more witty repartee with them. I completely ignored the people who didn't look well-off.

Turns out, that was a huge mistake. Most of the well-dressed people I thought would buy more stuff rarely did. Sometimes they would. Sometimes they wouldn't. I was always surprised when the "poor looking people" would drop several hundred dollars without batting an eyelash.

I learned very quickly that if I was going to allow what I thought about people to affect how I treated them, my payday was going to suffer. It's only when I finally stopped behaving in a prejudiced way, and allowed myself to just do the show for everybody with respect, that my sales started getting better.

We like to think we're all virtuous people for completely altruistic reasons, but sometimes it takes dollars and cents not to be a jerk.

Jonathan **Pritchard**

Back to the lesson.

We can't get rid of our emotions (nor should we want to), but we can question the validity of what we believe they're trying to tell us. When you get into the habit of questioning your beliefs, you'll stop thinking in absolutes. You'll use "always" and "never" less often. You'll stop having one bad experience with a single person and then think "Everyone is like that!" You'll stop berating yourself as much. You won't say, "I'll never be able to do that!"

Instead, you'll allow yourself to ask if it's actually true, and you'll discover that while you're frustrated now, that doesn't mean it's how it's always going to be. This is a much more freeing approach to life. Give yourself the permission and space to make change, and you'll be surprised how much positive change you can make!

At this point you might be having doubts that it's this simple. You're thinking, "I don't do that!" If that's the case, I'd like to introduce you to a friend of mine named "rationalization." It's your friend too. We all do it.

We have an experience, feel a certain way about it, tell ourselves what that means, and then justify our position with logic. This is the natural sequence.

The sequence we buy into, however, is that something

happens, we think about it, come to a logical conclusion, and then respond appropriately.

Nonsense. Rationalization is a defense mechanism to accommodate unhealthy, antisocial, or flat-out wrong behaviors to avoid the difficult job of owning up to that behavior. And it happens mostly on the subconscious level, but it happens usually to avoid shame or guilt. We think we know ourselves better than we do, so we lie to ourselves about who we truly are. This is called the self-serving bias.

We tend to ascribe success to our own abilities, but our failures to external circumstances beyond our control. We are prejudiced to focus more on our strengths than our weakness. If someone else is late to a meeting, it's because they don't respect your time and consequently are a moral failure; but if you're late to a meeting, it's because there was crazy traffic on 5th Avenue! If you get a good grade on a test it's because you're the smartest person on the face of the planet. If you get a bad grade, it's because the instructor is lousy at teaching.

The first step to mitigating the negative effects of rationalization and prejudice is recognizing that it's happening, even though you might not have noticed it before. This will help you think more clearly; and the more clearly you think, the fewer opportunities your mind has to lie to itself (you).

We all have the tendency to believe what we want to believe. After all, that's part of being human, right? But the important part is recognizing that wanting something to be so doesn't mean it is. When this hits home for you, you'll be one step closer to freedom.

Kill Your Habits Before They Kill You

Earlier I mentioned how our mental model of how the world works is installed relatively early in life. This goes for relationship dynamics, the strategies we use to get our needs met by our caregivers, the amount of self-confidence we have, and more.

What you think about all these things seems so obviously true mainly because it's the way you've done it for so long. Imagine you've been doing a task one way for thirty years, only to be shown a better way to do it. How likely would you be to change? You'd probably tell yourself, "My way's not all that bad. It's worked well enough this way so far." The way you've always done it is poor justification for mediocrity. That's the power habit uses to kill you.

Most of your thoughts fall into a narrow range of possibility mainly because that's just how you grew up doing it. Your friends think the same way, your parents think the same way, your teachers taught you to think the same way, so of course you think the same way as everyone else.

The way you do things when you think for yourself tends to be distinctly different from the majority, but you don't have to be different just for the sake of being different. But learning to accept it if you are is time well spent. The way I make a living is completely unimaginable to most people, but I still use a knife and fork to eat like everyone else.

The heart of the matter is that we have to question everything in order to think effectively. This doesn't mean you have to be overly critical, demoralizing, or cynical. It's more about encouraging a general inquisitiveness about why things are the way they are, and being comfortable straying from the usual path if it leads you somewhere you don't want to be.

Not all of your habits and beliefs are good ones. Take the time to examine what they are, why they are the way they are, and whether or not you could achieve the same goals with better habits in the future. You might be convinced that your beliefs and behaviors are the best they can be. I can appreciate that. Remember, however, that the level of conviction you have about something has zero correlation to how right it is. Realize that suicide bombers have total conviction; it doesn't make them right.

To me, it takes more courage to question your beliefs, and to sometimes admit they're wrong rather than dying for them. There's no shame in admitting you're wrong. In fact, it's one of the first signs of making positive change. It's uncomfortable at first, but just remind yourself that even the smartest people through history have admitted they know nothing. Pretty sure Socrates would have been a great drinking buddy. Don't have what he's having, though.

Chapter 5: Hello Spock - An Introduction to Logic

In the fully automated luxury gay space communism utopia propaganda piece known as Star Trek, my favorite character is Spock, a creature born of Human-Vulcan relations.

His mother was human and represents the more emotionally driven side of things, while his father was Vulcan and stands for logic and reason. Throughout the many years of the TV show and various movie appearances, this tension between emotions and reason helps us feel a lot of sympathy for his situation. How often do we ourselves feel torn between our head and our hearts?

Turns out, they don't have to be at odds with each other. Once you understand how logic works, and how to think through things in a logically consistent fashion, nobody will be able to control you based purely on emotional appeals.

This doesn't mean going 100 percent Vulcan and ignoring your emotional side. Rather, learning how to use logic to understand the heart of an issue will give your emotional systems more accurate information to respond to.

This chapter will be dedicated to outlining how logic works, how it applies to everyday situations, and how it can be led astray, with personal examples from my experiences peppered throughout.

What I want to avoid, though, is an exhaustive study of logic. There are entire college courses devoted to traditional logic, symbolic logic, complex dilemmas, and on and on. Here, we're going to mostly focus on what I like to call practical philosophy; stuff we can actually use! This typically means logic as applied to ethics.

Logic breaks down into two parts: 1) epistemology, which is an examination of what differentiates opinion from justified belief, the nature of what's true, and the theory of knowledge; and 2) dialectics, which is the art of investigating the truth of opinions. We'll be focusing quite a bit on dialectics because it is how we figure out the right ways of thinking so that we can get to the truth of an issue.

Dialectics are important because plenty of people have opinions about stuff that are in no way connected with reality. You can have whatever opinions you want, but if they're demonstrably false, they're not going to do much for you.

When you look into dialectics, you'll figure out there are three main areas: simple apprehension, judgement, and reasoning.

Simple apprehension basically means being aware of something. Your mind is attending to an object, or thing, and that's it. "This is a fruit" would be an example of simple apprehension.

Judgements are basically the combination of two simple apprehensions that are talking about the same thing; so to continue the example above, a judgement would be not just thinking "this is a fruit" but "this is a green fruit." If you see someone and think to yourself, "This is a woman," that's a simple apprehension; but if you think, "This is a beautiful woman," then you've made a judgement.

In the same way that judgements are the combination of two simple apprehensions, reasoning consists of two judgements pertaining to some thing, person, or idea. If your reasoning leads to a third judgement, we call that a conclusion.

This is a fantastic book. (First Judgement)
I enjoy reading this book. (Second Judgement)
Therefore... (Reasoning)
I enjoy reading fantastic books. (Conclusion)

Correct Thinking

The process of reasoning can go two ways. The first is often called "bottom up" reasoning. We start with our individual experiences, then use logic to form broader ideas about how the world works. This is also traditionally called induction.

And then there's the "top down" approach. That's when you take general principles and work down to specific details. This is traditionally called deduction.

At this point I'm not going to talk about induction. Instead, we're going to focus on deduction. This is because most of us use deduction all day, every day without ever realizing it! If you don't know how it works, you're more likely to make some rookie mistakes that will cost you dearly when you think through a problem.

The example I mentioned at the end of the previous section is a type of deductive reasoning that you might already be familiar with: a syllogism. That's the fancy term for the act of inferring a new judgement or conclusion from two previous judgements. Here's another example:

1. All men are mortal.
2. I am a man.
3. Therefore I am mortal.

This is a rather clunky example, but it's good to start with the basics. You can see that it's simply the process of saying "Because this and this (the two judgements) are true, therefore that (the conclusion) is also true."

A syllogism is always three distinct steps, but most people think of the first two steps as two parts of a single process; and sometimes all three are one, too.

Even if you don't consciously realize you're using them, you're doing it nonstop. And it stands to reason that if you aren't even aware you're doing something, it's likely you're not doing it properly. This is the heart of most of your bad thinking.

You can go astray with a wrong premise, or an incorrect judgement in step 1 or 2. You can make the mistake of using a specific instance to "prove" a generalization. If you do that, you're making the mistake of swapping out "all" for "some." This is the heart of stereotypes and racism, by the way. The reasoning process might be rock solid, but you'll still wind up with false conclusions.

Without even trying that hard, you can probably think up lots of examples for each of those pitfalls.

1. If the street is wet, it has rained recently. (Faulty Premise: It could've recently been cleaned)
2. The street is wet. (True)
3. Therefore it has rained recently. (False Conclusion)

1. He was a Jedi. (True)
2. Now he's a Sith. (True)
3. Therefore all Jedi are Sith. (False Conclusion: Too general a statement)

And over-generalization doesn't have to be in the conclusion to wreck your reasoning. It can do just as bad a job in one of the first judgements, too.

1. All mentalists are hacks. (False: Too general a statement)
2. I am a mentalist. (True)
3. Therefore I am a hack. (False Conclusion)

Hopefully, if you've seen me perform you'll realize that's faulty reasoning. If you do, however, agree with that reasoning, you're committing the pitfall of taking a single example to prove a generality!

Your Mental Scorecard

How does your reasoning stack up? Do you realize now that you've often been making simple mistakes? To err is human, right?! We're not Vulcan. We haven't been trained from birth to think in purely logical terms. We go with what feels right, often at the expense of accuracy and truth.

There are even more fun ways of getting it wrong! You can sometimes have the right conclusion, but have faulty logic that got you there.

1. All animals eat meat.
2. Dogs are animals.
3. Therefore dogs eat meat.

You can see how your conclusion is 100 percent accurate, but your thinking would have been way off-base. This is a challenge to organized thinking. When you're dealing with subjects you know inside and out, it's not as easy to fall for this kind of trap. It's when we're dealing with unfamiliar subjects that it becomes easy to make these syllogistic mistakes. If you're not an expert on the topic you're thinking about, keep your mental guard up if you want to preserve your ability to think effectively!

Here's an example of what I mean. I'm going to present you with two syllogisms, and you tell me which is easiest to recognize as faulty logic. Are they both wrong? If so, which one took less time for you to realize it was wrong?

1. All X's are Y's.
2. All Z's are Y's.
3. Therefore some X's are Z's.

1. All dogs are animals.
2. All cats are animals.
3. Therefore some dogs are cats.

These two syllogisms are structurally identical, but the second is easier to recognize as being wrong. You knew it wasn't correct as soon as you read the third part. As for the first syllogism, you might still be making your mind up about it. If that was the case with you, you now have first-hand experience with the point I'm making.

Dogs and cats are well-known to you. You're familiar with them. They're not an abstract idea. You've probably petted at least one in your life. Letters, however, are symbolic. They're not real. In the first syllogism the letters stood for something that you weren't really 100 percent sure of. In fact, they could stand for anything really, even things that would make the conclusion correct; but it still doesn't change the fact that the process of logic is broken in the example.

The lesson is, when you use syllogistic reasoning, make sure to check the facts, verify the information, and make double sure you know what in the world you're talking about in all three parts of the syllogism. You might think I'm belaboring the point with basic examples—and I am—but the point still stands. These examples are an easy starting place with topics that are familiar to you, to help you better understand where your thinking goes off the rails. Now that you understand the simple concept, it's up to you to make sure your logic is up to Vulcan standards.

Wrong On Purpose

After seeing how easy it is to make mistakes, it would be a good idea to not take things for granted. Don't repost something on Facebook just because it says what you want to be true. Don't believe something just because you heard it said with confidence repeatedly by others. Remember, when a lie is heard often, your tendency is to believe it even more strongly!

Nowhere can you see logic thrown out the window with more reckless abandon than in the world of advertising. There's a heavy reliance on a logical fallacy known as "appeal to authority." In pure syllogistic terms it looks like this:

1. X is an expert on subject Y.
2. X claims fact A based on subject Y.
3. Therefore, fact A is true.

The problem is, in the world of advertising, the "expert" on subject Y is usually an actor who is not an expert at all, but is an expert at saying things with a sense of authority.

You can see this all the time in the world of diet fads. Actors and actresses advocate whatever diet-of-the-month they're on, and thousands of people hop on the train without a second thought of how healthy the diet actually is. They think:

1. The actor seems fit.
2. They eat this way.
3. Therefore if I eat this way, I'll be fit too.

But as we've seen before, judgement 1 is a faulty premise; it's actually supremely difficult to evaluate someone's overall health just by looking at them, no matter how convincingly they say otherwise.

Want a more drastic example? Think back to the time when 9 out of 10 doctors smoked Camel brand cigarettes. There was a massive advertising campaign centered around the specious syllogism that since doctors know what's bad for you, and since they smoke Camels, therefore Camels must not be bad. They also got celebrities of the day to endorse Camels. Millions of dollars were spent so they would be seen in public holding Camel cigarettes, even if they didn't smoke!

Why do people fall for that? The only thing people know for sure is that the actor is famous. Everything beyond that is questionable. If you genuinely think every celebrity who endorses a product actually uses it, I have a bridge in New York I'd love to sell you. Further than that, even if the actor really did use everything he endorses, why on Earth would you think he's an expert in evaluating its quality? He might be an excellent actor but an awful judge of Thighmaster®.

The answer to all those questions is depressingly simple. We're intellectually lazy. Our brains have evolved to look for the simple answer. Our brains run on less electricity than the lightbulb in your fridge; there have to be corners cut somewhere. We prefer the path of least resistance; and when someone provides a simple answer, we prefer that to the hard work of evaluating our own beliefs, ideas, and the claims of others. Say anything with enough confidence, and people will believe you!

Now, don't get me wrong. I'm not saying we should do away with advertising. If you have something to sell the world, you have to tell folks about it. Marketers are doing their job, and they're doing a fine job of it. What you should notice, though, is how they're experts at manipulating the fundamental psychological systems that govern how you make decisions. Their methods will hijack your reasoning faculties, and lead you to conclusions that are nowhere near reality.

Think about how often you hear commercials for twenty different brands of the same product all claiming to be "THE BEST." Or it's now "25 percent less." Less than what?! Or, a fad that makes me laugh out loud; "Now Gluten Free." That's appearing on all sorts of products that never had gluten in the first place. It's a brilliant piece of marketing, and a terrible example of logical thinking. The point is, you absolutely must question assumptions (yours and anyone making a claim) if you want to make sure you're not led astray by faulty thinking. Faulty syllogisms will be your downfall otherwise. Do your own thinking, do your own research, and make your own [logically consistent] conclusions. Make Spock proud.

Secret to All Magic

I wanted to get through all that stuff to get to this; the explanation of every single magic trick you'll ever see. I've never heard it put like this, and there's a lot of thinking behind it. Here goes.

"The magician creates a context for logical assumptions that are later shown to not be true."

The magician: the agent of action. This is the person who is creating the experience for the audience. Nothing is left to chance. From start to finish, this is the person who has thought through the entire experience, and practiced every day to make sure there's no hint of how he's doing what you're watching him do. Sometimes that can take years of dedicated practice before a routine is performed in public.

Creates a context: Everything the magician does contributes to building a mental framework that the audience uses to understand what they're seeing.

Nothing is unimportant. The physical space (theater, Tarot card parlour, casual setting, on the street, etc), the words he uses, his movements, everything he doesn't say/do, and so on.

We never understand anything out of context, so the magician consciously builds an experiential framework through an imperceptible mix of truth and falsehoods (verbal and otherwise) that will help people make assumptions about what's really going on. He literally has to see his actions through your eyes. He puts himself in your position, and imagines what you're thinking at every step through the trick. This is the power of empathy, and it's a superpower no other creature on the planet possesses. And we take it for granted. Being able to understand what someone else is experiencing, and then use that knowledge to modify our behavior to achieve a specific outcome, is simply mind-blowing to me. Yet we do it all the time when we talk to someone, try to understand why our sweetie is upset, or read the emotions of a stranger on the bus.

For Logical Assumptions: You make assumptions about the world all the time. You assume the ground will support you as you walk. You assume your coffee mug isn't going to suddenly float off your desk. Without these mental shortcuts we'd never get out of bed in the morning! These beliefs about the rules that govern reality are based on your years of previous experiences, and on paying attention to what does and does not happen in your world. Your mind then makes logical predictions about the future based on your experiences from the past.

Since you know gravity works 100 percent of the time, you assume that (in this context) the coin in the magician's palm dropped out when he turned it over. Your assumption about gravity, combined with the seamless way he performed the sleight of hand needed to keep the coin palmed, makes it a logical assumption that the coin is now somewhere else.

This point explains why magic and mentalism doesn't work for children all that well. They lack the required life experience to understand what is and isn't possible in reality. Nor do they have well-developed logical faculties. They already live in a world of imagination and infinite possibility. Nobody has told them yet what can't be done, so magic isn't any different from how they view the world already. Fantastic stuff is happening all the time when you're a kid! So, without logical assumptions, there's no magical effect. As an adult, however, you trust your logical assumptions implicitly; and the stronger you believe in them, the stronger the magical effect is.

That are later shown to not be true: You've been watching like a hawk, and you know exactly what's going on. You didn't blink once, and that magician didn't get away with anything. You know right where that coin is! But he slowly opens both hands to show them completely empty. The coin has vanished! Your logical assumptions about where the coin currently exists are demonstrably wrong. That's why the potential amazement you'll feel at the end of a magic trick is directly related to the amount you're certain about what you're seeing. Most magicians will tell you that confusion and magic don't mix. If you're confused, you're thinking "I must have missed something" and you won't be amazed. If, however, you're paying close attention, when the coin disappears, that's magic!

Just like in logic, the same is true for magic. When you're surprised at an outcome, you have to question your assumptions that you're probably not even aware that you're making! Good luck catching the magician though. They've been working at this lying stuff for thousands of years, and have spent their life getting good at using your logical faculties for their gain. This is the biggest secret in magic, and the psychological process it's all built on. When you truly understand this process, you'll begin to see how many ways you fool yourself in your everyday life.

Expand Your Reality

Your experience is defined by your vocabulary. If you want to multiply your mind power, become a logophile.

The process of "thinking" isn't relegated only to images and pictures. Most of the time when we're thinking, we're actually talking to ourselves. Think about children who talk non-stop. As a parent, you wait it out for a couple years until you finally ask them to maybe be quiet for a moment. Their outer stream-of-consciousness babbling doesn't magically turn off. It instead merely turns inward where it continues for the rest of your life. So the conversations you can have with yourself are limited by the words you know. The ideas you could possibly come up with are limited by the words you know. Want to improve your potential? Improve your vocabulary.

The more words you're familiar with, the easier it will be for you to think accurately. Growing up I was often made fun of for using unnecessarily big words; but my love of words, their origins and their uses, has afforded me the requisite fodder for creative solutions to otherwise impossible-to-solve dilemmas. How did I get such a big vocabulary? Reading, of course. I grew up in a house with so many books, we sometimes had bookshelves in the bathroom! Any time I'd see a word I didn't know I'd immediately go look it up in the dictionary. Nowadays, it's even easier. Just highlight the text, right-click, and choose "Search Google for. . ."

This is also where the power of concentration really pays off. How often have you been reading an article only to realize halfway through that you haven't a clue what it's about? Your mind checked out a long time ago! Maybe it's happened here already?

The trick is to learn how to enjoy reading and learning at the same time. Challenge yourself with the type of material you choose to read. Do you tend to pick the tabloids at the grocery store checkout line that are written for a 5th grade reading level? Or do you pick biographies of great historical figures and events? Do you try to get inside the minds of the movers and shakers of history, and glean every last bit of genius they have hidden between the lines? You always make time for what's important, and if you haven't made time for improving your vocabulary, now is as good a time as any.

Remember. If you're going to talk to yourself, you might as well have an educated discussion.

Mental Exercises

Not only can you read good books to flex your brain power, you can practice all sorts of mental exercises to get your mind in shape. Creative problem-solving is a skill just like anything else, and if you want to get better at it, you have to practice! Have you ever solved a crossword puzzle? Have you ever tried a crossword puzzle? You might not get too many clues on your first attempt, but once you put in consistent effort, you'll be amazed at how many you can figure out. Crossword puzzles, specifically, are a good mental exercise because they will improve your vocabulary. Check the answers for the clues you didn't solve, and you'll probably run into a couple words you've never seen before. Plus, they're full of puns and questions that require you to "think around corners" as my grandpa always told me to do.

If you're shy like me and looking for a way to get over it, charades are a great party game that will get your brain working. Everyone takes a slip of paper and writes a word, action, or (if they want to be really difficult) idea. They fold it up and put it into a hat. Whoever goes next chooses a slip, reads what's on it to themselves, and acts out the word without saying anything until someone can figure out what the word is. It's a challenging game, and a fun time with the right people.

Riddles are another fun pastime that can put your brain power to the test. Also known as "solve-ems," they require you to take yourself out of your familiar ways of thinking and approach the question with a unique perspective. Here are some fun questions to get you started.

1. Johnny's mother had three children. The first child was named April. The second child was named May. What was the third child's name?

2. A clerk at a butcher shop stands five feet ten inches tall and wears size 13 sneakers. What does he weigh?

3. Before Mt. Everest was discovered, what was the highest mountain in the world?

4. How much dirt is there in a hole that measures two feet by three feet by four feet?

5. What word in the English language is always spelled incorrectly?

6. Billie was born on December 28th, yet her birthday always falls in the summer. How is this possible?

7. In British Columbia you cannot take a picture of a man with a wooden leg. Why not?

8. If you were running a race and you passed the person in 2nd place, what place would you be in now?

9. Which is correct to say, "The yolk of the egg is white" or "The yolk of the egg are white?"

10. A farmer has five haystacks in one field and four haystacks in another. How many haystacks would he have if he combined them all in one field?

There are also plenty of apps that claim to improve your brain function. They usually focus on addressing your memory, attention, problem solving, and so on. A word of caution, however. While all these things are fun, and get your brain out of a rut, there's not much evidence that the specific skillsets you're practicing will transfer to other situations. In other words, if you get really good at a memory game in an app, it's likely that you're getting good at that memory game instead of improving your overall memory. We'll go over tricks on how to do that later!

The point is, if you don't take time to challenge your thinking skills, they're going to atrophy like any other skill or muscle. It's important to maintain your abilities when the stakes are low so that you'll have the ability to handle situations when the stakes are at their highest.

Riddle Answers:

1. Johnny.
2. Meat.
3. Mt. Everest. It just wasn't discovered yet.
4. There is no dirt in a hole.
5. Incorrectly (except when it is spelled incorrecktly).
6. Billie lives in the southern hemisphere.
7. You can't take a picture with a wooden leg. You need a camera (or iPad or cell phone) to take a picture.
8. You would be in 2nd place. You passed the person in second place, not first.
9. Neither. Egg yolks are yellow.
10. One. If he combines all his haystacks, they all become one big stack.

Chapter 6: I Wish I Were Creative

Success is impossible without creativity, and if I had a dollar for every time I've had someone tell me, "I wish I were creative," I'd be able to retire tomorrow. Creativity is a slippery thing to talk about, but I'm going to do my best to be as clear, specific, and concrete as I can.

Creativity is a skill, just like everything else we've been talking about. It's not just something you're born with; it's something you have to keep at to maintain. Sound familiar? So how can I teach you something you've chosen to forget? You've had years and possibly decades to convince yourself you don't have it.

But you do.

The fastest way I could teach you to improve your imagination is to get you to just go ahead and be more imaginative! Allow yourself to say, "I'm creative!" Have the audacity to recognize you've already found creative solutions to many of your problems. Just because they don't look like what you think they should look like doesn't mean they aren't. You have to practice, just like anything else. Haven't felt confident in a long time? It'll take work. Haven't been kind in a long time? It'll take work. If you put in the work of being creative, I promise you, you'll discover a fountain of creativity that's always been there waiting for you to come back.

Nowadays we don't have to be too creative. We have push-button solutions to our problems, and any question of fact we have can be answered in .02 seconds on Wikipedia. But our lives are more than the facts. Most people would rather climb Mount Everest than expend the least amount of mental effort. We'd prefer others to do our thinking for us. We'd rather repaint the whole house than actually sit down and work on that idea we have for the next Great American Novel. Invention requires thinking.

But think about this. Every single human advancement throughout history has been the result of our imagination. Every single thing created by human hands had to, first, be conceived in the human mind. Then it is made real through physical effort. Every discovery. Every innovation. Every new technology is the result of human ingenuity. Not a single thing is possible without it, and it is the most essential element we're the most lacking in.

Maybe She's Born With It, Maybe It's Creativity

You realize creativity is important, and you'd like to be more creative. I get it. You also think you have to be born with it, or you don't have it. I would agree with you, but go one step farther. You were. Everybody is born creative. How often have you had the chance to talk with a child? You'll notice right away they are full of the most off-the-wall imaginative ideas you could ever hope for. They live and breathe a world of endless possibility. But, over time they seem to lose it. It happened to you, and it happened to almost everyone you know.

What incredible discoveries or works of art have been kept from the world due to your losing that playful side of your personality? No wonder you tell yourself you're not creative; to accept responsibility for letting it go is too difficult. Telling yourself you never had it in the first place is easier to accept.

The good news, however, is that it's not gone forever. It's patiently waiting for you. It's not a special gift bestowed only to the professional artists amongst us. If you want it, put in the work to uncover it, and you'll discover a treasure you've had all along. How, then, should you get started? We've already covered some of the basics like cultivating your enthusiasm, curiosity, and interest. Each is a component of being creative. Once you tune into each of those, you'll immediately be aware of so many little details about life you've rarely noticed before. These make the best fodder for creative projects. Think about it. Collages made from magazines have hung in the finest art galleries and museums. The medium is plain, but it's the attention to detail that gives birth to the creative work. Any off-handed remark, chance encounter, or random thought could lead you to making the next big thing. J.K. Rowling had the idea for Harry Potter while she was delayed on a train in 1990. Now she's worth millions and millions of dollars. Used to be billions, but she donated most of it to charities.

Distractions Are Not Your Friend

I love being bored. It's when I get my best thinking done. But it's difficult to be bored if you're distracted all the time. With the most interesting human invention (the internet-ready cellphone) within arm's reach at all times, it's easy to never feel a moment's boredom.

Have you ever stopped to wonder why your best ideas come to you in the shower? It's because it's boring in there! You have nothing distracting you, so your brain has to entertain itself. This is why I love driving to shows if I have the time. I like to call it "Strategic Boredom." I've routinely driven 12 to 14 hours in one day with no radio or audiobooks to distract me; just me and the road. Nobody can walk up to my desk and interrupt me. I don't have to chat with the person sitting next to me like I would on the plane. It's just me alone with my thoughts. It isn't long before my mind can't stand the silence and starts coming up with all kinds of ideas in an attempt to entertain itself.

Where do you think I had the idea for writing this

book? In the middle of a Strategic Boredom Session!

Excuses Kill Creativity

Stop telling yourself there's nothing new under the sun. You sound like the Commissioner of the US Patent Office, Charles H. Duell, who supposedly once said, "Everything that can be invented has been invented." He sure got that wrong! There are limitless ideas to explore. New approaches to try. Imagination is the only way to get ahead nowadays.

Take Elon Musk, for example. He invented PayPal. SpaceX. Tesla motors. Solar powered batteries. He's working on the HyperLoop. Boring a multilevel tunnel system under Los Angeles.

We had online payments. He came up with a better way to do it. We've had rockets before. He made better ones. We've had tunnels before. He's making better ones. It takes a phenomenal imagination to bring the level of creativity that's he's spending on tunnels. Case in point, he's trying to develop a tunnel digging machine that can outpace a snail.

And it's making his companies worth billions and billions of dollars.

You don't have to come up with a reusable rocket to be creative. No, you can start right where you are, and what you're already working on. Most of my life my dad worked in factories. One in particular I can remember was a factory for interior doors. They would break down wood chips into simple fibers and then mix them with resin before putting them in a huge hydraulic press. In goes the fiber/resin mix, and out comes a "door skin;" a thin sheet that looks like wood grain that would be assembled into a lightweight interior door.

As with any system of mass production, there were bound to be flaws. There would be wood chips that weren't broken down enough, so there would be little slivers of wood sticking up from the surface. This would scratch other skins as they moved through the assembly process, so it was important to catch as many of the flawed skins as possible. The problem was, they're all the same color with a wood texture pattern, so it's difficult to spot.

They had an employee incentive program for any suggestions that improved the quality of their work, and dad came up with a clever idea that was as effective as it was simple. He suggested they position lights at an oblique angle to the skins as they came out of the press. This means any imperfections in the skin would cast a long shadow which was much easier to see than the flaw itself. It was an inexpensive solution that saved the company thousands and thousands of dollars by preventing future problems. That little bit of creativity earned him a bonus check that was much appreciated.

That's the power of a good idea. A single suggestion can improve an entire industry! Sure, most of the ideas people drop in the box aren't going to be great, but every once in awhile you get a real winner. It's a simple numbers game, so churn out as many run-of-the-mill ideas as you can to get to the occasional gem.

Don't wait for the bonus. Create as many constructive ideas as you can. Good ideas will get you paid more, establish better working conditions, and provide the satisfaction of knowing you've made a positive difference in the world. There's nothing much better than seeing one of your ideas in action. And this can apply to every area of your life.

6 Degrees of Psychic Kevin Bacon

There's a game I play during my show that nobody else knows is going on, and I call it "6 Degrees of Psychic Kevin Bacon." The idea is, just like you can get from any actor to Kevin Bacon in six steps or less, I can get to your thought in six associations or less. No matter what your word / thought / idea is, and no matter where I start, I can get there by free association in six steps or less. You may not see how the beginning correlates to the ending, but that process of connecting those dots are a phenomenally powerful exercise in creativity. It takes some serious sideways thinking skills and a little imagination to connect two completely separate ideas. For example: How would you correlate "toothpick" with "speedboat?" Toothpick -- items that come in boxes -- matches -- cigarette -- cigarette speedboat. We've done it in five steps.

This is how it looks in the show. I already know what word my volunteer has in his mind by secret methods unknown to him or the audience. I'll throw out any word, idea, or concept that comes to mind first that has nothing to do with where I'm going to wind up. In the speedboat example I'd say, "Are you thinking of toothpick? Does that make sense?" And he would say "No." I then say, "It's nothing that comes in a little box? Like, maybe matches?" He says "No." I then say, "Because, in my mind, I'm seeing you light a cigarette. Does that make sense?" If he is thinking of a cigarette speedboat, he'll smile, laugh, and then say, "Oh, yeah! That makes sense!" Now it looks like I knew what he was thinking about better than he does, and it took him awhile to catch up to me. I get credit for knowing his mind better than he does! It's a great exercise, and you can practice it on your own by making associations between completely different things.

This is the essence of creativity; seeing connections that nobody else sees.

Creativity Multipliers

If connections are the rocket fuel for creativity, here are the nitro boosters you can add to the mix for even more good ideas. Question everything. Ask why until you get to "I don't know" and start digging. Use exaggeration.

These approaches will always get you something you've never thought about before. Simply looking for answers can jumpstart your creative juices. Once you find the answer to one thing, you'll learn about something you've never heard of, and then use that as a jumping off point to find new connections. Don't pre-edit your inquiry, either. That's your critical mind talking, and criticism is the sworn enemy of creativity. Sometimes the stupidest question can get you the smartest answers.

Also note that the answers are the least interesting part of this equation. The general inquisitiveness about how the world works, why people do what they do, what's going on under the hood, are all more interesting questions than they are definitive statements. So, don't get wrapped up in always having an answer. Be like Socrates. Be okay knowing that you don't know things. You're still farther ahead after asking the question than you were beforehand.

Don't be disappointed if you aren't making breakthroughs every day. Being creative is often a very boring affair. It's hard work. It's dull work. I'll tell you right now that most of the things people compliment me on about my show is the result of countless hours spent turning an idea over and over in my mind. It's not much to look at, but the results are astounding. Stick-to-it-tiveness is the essential ingredient. Plodding along without being discouraged will get you the results you're looking for. Make it a habit to finish what you start. Don't just rely on your momentary whim to accomplish anything; great things take concerted effort. Not wishing and praying.

I've experienced this firsthand while writing this book. It's infinitely easier to not write the book. There are a million reasons not to do anything. In order to finish I'm focusing on the single reason to write it: it might help you. Now I have a moral obligation not to stop! Same goes for you. You have a moral obligation to be as creative and full of life as you can; if not for yourself, then for everyone you can inspire, even if you're a spectacular failure.

You don't have to be perfect to inspire people. Sometimes it's how we handle our failures that help others the most. Did you start writing a book? Finish it. Did you start a painting three years ago? Finish it. Did you sign up for improv classes but never go? Do it. Want to redecorate your apartment? Do it. I don't care what it is you've been putting off. Just do it. Taking action will always beat the perfect idea anyday.

A weird thing happens when you come back to something you've abandoned. Sometimes it's not as worthless as you thought when you left it. With your new experiences you have new ways of seeing your old work. Your improved eye will see the merits you missed previously. So, the more creative action you take, the more creative potential you'll have for your next try.

Don't let fear tell you to stop. Most people I talk to are too embarrassed to own their creativity. They're scared to come up with something new. Even then, assuming they do take the leap to create something, they lack the confidence to follow through with it. But that's their story. Not yours. You take action. You get things done. You listen to your own good ideas.

The limits on your life are the limits on your imagination. Free your mind, and you free yourself.

Chapter 7: Make Time for Success

One of my favorite parts of high school chemistry class was stoichiometry; the process of balancing equations. Essentially, you'd have to figure out how much of a chemical you would need to ensure there's none left over at the end of a chemical reaction.

This requires you to convert units of measurement, like gallons to liters, or grams to ounces. Most people hated it because, well, it involves math. What interested me, though, is how the material didn't change, only how we measured it.

The same goes for your life. Whether you're spending dollars or effort the only measurement that counts is time.

All of us have the same 24 hours in a day. Nobody is born with more than that. We don't have "rollover" minutes. We can't borrow time, or give time back. We can't save time. It can only be spent. So invest it the right way on the right things. How much time have you invested in yourself mentally and physically? How much time have you spent on improving your skills?

Almost everyone complains about how they don't have enough time. How they're so busy. How they wish they could take care of themselves, but they have to do X, Y, or Z first. They're thinking about time completely wrong. When you focus on what you "have to do," you're telling yourself you're not in control of how you spend your time. Instead, try asking yourself, "What's most important to me? What do I want to happen by the end of my time here?" This will help you focus on the results you want, think about whether or not they're important to you, and then spend time on things you want to do. You'll quickly realize you're able to get a lot more done in a much shorter time.

That's why I believe that the old saying is 100 percent true, that if you want something done, ask a person who is too busy. A person who makes the most of their time realizes the virtue of not letting things pile up. They take action immediately.

The more you want to accomplish, the more important organization and economy of motion will become to you. My friend CJ Johnson is a master at this. When he has a repetitious task ahead of him, he will spend the time to figure out how to complete it with the fewest moves possible, and then do them as quickly as he can. He makes a game out of it, and he gets more done in a single day than most people can in a month. He realizes time is too valuable a commodity to not get the most out of it that he can. After seeing him in action I truly believe that anyone who says they don't have time for something is simply not organizing their time effectively.

Two Thieves of Time

If you want your time back, you have to face procrastination and indecision. Both are quietly stealing your time right under your nose. You're missing out on opportunities, experiencing more problems, and getting left behind because you take too long making up your mind. Indecision will paralyze you. I know from experience. My ex-wife told me once, "Indecision is a decision." And she's right. Indecision is refusing to take responsibility for your life. It's telling yourself that everybody else is better qualified to make your choices than you are. That is not how you go about building the best life. That was a hard lesson for me to learn, but one I'm glad I figured out. I'd rather not have to spend any more time than I have to on that one!

Indecision usually happens when you don't see a good way forward. You don't like any of the options you can see, so you think waiting it out by not choosing any of them is your best bet. But, as she said, "Indecision is a decision." It's a decision to let precious time slip through your fingers. I'm here to tell you that making mistakes is a thousand percent better than not making a decision.

The faster you make the mistake, the more time you'll have to fix it. But you won't know what you need to work on until you take action. I don't care which direction you choose so long as you get started. Only then can you build momentum, and figure out which way you should be moving.

I used to spend way too much time on things that didn't actually make a difference in my life. That's why one of my New Year's resolutions was to never match my socks again. Now I just grab two socks in the morning, and whatever they are I wear them. Don't get me wrong, I won't go out of my way to unmatch my socks; I just won't spend time finding their mate. That's time I could spend reading, learning, or relaxing with someone I love.

I've talked with a lot of people about how they spend their time, and most folks waste too much time on the stuff that just doesn't matter. Like, trying to decide on what restaurant to go to. Or whether to take the bus or an Uber. Or buy this one, or the other that's two dollars more expensive. On down the rabbithole of time-wasting it goes.

I've helped avoid most of that with this simple rule. If it's a question that doesn't involve money, I do whatever is easiest for me. That might sound selfish, but there you have it. I've now saved hours and hours of time formerly spent hemming and hawing about what I should do. Now I have a general rule to depend on! In the grand scheme of things, the questions I answer with that rule just aren't worth spending any longer than that on. Make the choice, and move on. Done.

When money is involved, it only changes a little. If we're talking very little difference in dollar amounts, I'll again go with what's easiest. Larger sums require more consideration, but it has to be worth it. Remember, time is money, right? And if you spend days or weeks thinking about a couple hundred dollars, you've been penny smart and a pound foolish. Set your own limits based on your own financial situation; just realize that you can always get more money but you'll never get more time. This will help you focus your time on things that actually matter.

Most people who say they're too busy to do the important things are more interested in feeling busy instead of actually accomplishing things. They prefer to procrastinate by working on projects that don't get them any closer to their goals. They're busy, but not productive. That is the most egregious misuse of time I can think of! They're spending their time wishing for things they could have if they spent their time actively instead.

If you want to achieve something, do something about

it. There's never going to be a right time. The best time is now. You're always going to find a reason not to take action. Don't believe it! Those excuses will kill your dreams. You have to train yourself not to focus on the urgent things at the expense of the important things. Stop spending your time navel-gazing about whether or not you should do that thing, and focus instead on how you're going to get it done. Then get it done!

I've been around too many people in my life who spent countless hours talking about the things they could do, who never spent one minute towards actually doing them. There's a big difference between the talkers with no results, and people who let their results do all the talking for them. Which one are you?

Non-Newtonian Time

Before we talk about how to manage your time, I want to talk a little bit about the phrase that opened this chapter, "Make time." In the traditional sense, we all have the same amount of time, sure. A minute is a minute is a minute. It's part of physics. Cause and effect bound by Newton's laws of thermodynamics. But. Our experience of time is wildly variable. In some instances a minute feels like forever. Or hours go by in a flash, in what psychologist Mihaly Csikszentmihalyi terms the "flow state." My wild idea is that we actually make time. You are the source of the time you experience. If you're bored, you've made more time than you need. If you're anxious, you've made too little. You literally make time for the things you want to do; it's not a figure of speech. Making time is a skill. (How many times do I have to tell you life is a skill before you throw this book across the room?)

Let's look at how to sharpen your time-making abilities! The first question to ask yourself is whether or not you're consistently lacking enough time to get the important stuff done. If so, you haven't learned how to make enough time. If you're facing a mountain of work with too little time to do it, here's what you can do...

Try saying yes to fewer projects. Maybe you're bad at saying no, and would do well to give yourself a break. If you're like me, though, that's not a possibility. So here's what you do instead. Tackle the tasks that can get done later first. After those are done, then take on the do-or-die projects. What you're doing is essentially leveraging procrastination in your favor. You know that the things that absolutely have to get done will get done. The stuff that can wait is really what eats up your time. They wind up just sitting there, never going anywhere, which winds up eating at the back of your mind. This creates the feeling that you never can get anything done, and that you're constantly behind schedule. This leads to indecision, which holds everything up. So, the answer is simple. Get 'em done!

Chores and tasks are like a gas; they will expand to fill the time available for them. I experience this when I'm setting up my presentations. If I show up three hours early, set-up somehow takes three hours. If I show up with only 45 minutes to set up, I'm still ready to go exactly on time. It's a weird quirk of the human mind that we will find ways to fill the time we create for things. That's why if you put off the less urgent stuff to the end, you don't have the do-or-die projects behind them to keep you on your toes. If you do it the other way, strangely enough you'll find you have more time for the important stuff!

The second thing to do is ask yourself what you're actually interested in doing. If you're not actually interested in the work you have, it's no wonder you don't make time for it. We always make time for the things we want to do. Always. So, do you tell yourself you "have to" get this or that done? That makes you feel obligated to get it done, which leads to resentment. And how often are you happy to do something you're resentful of? Is it still a mystery why you don't make the time for it? Instead, remind yourself this is actually something you want to do. There's some reason you're motivated to get it done. It may not be to do it for its own sake, but there is a reason you're doing it; otherwise you would experience zero drive to accomplish it.

Another way to make more time for the important stuff is to create a system of habits for the unimportant stuff. Make the routine chores that you do on a regular basis a matter of habit. Do them the same way every time. I put my keys, phone, and wallet in exactly the same place every single night. I spend zero time looking for them because I've created a mindless habit to do so. If you try it, you'll be able to chores without thinking about them either, and your mind will be free to think about other things. This makes the most out of time which would be otherwise wasted. Another example of this would be using your commute to listen to an audiobook or a podcast. You have to get work anyway, so you're going to be spending that time one way or the other, right? Now, instead of listening to the radio, you'll be using these consistent chunks of time to invest in yourself.

Time Cushion

Let me introduce you to Hofstadter's Law: "It always takes longer than you expect, even when you take into account Hofstadter's Law." This is another way of saying that tasks are like a gas. You have to fight the tendency to let things fill up your time.

I used to schedule things to the exact minute. Google Maps says it takes 17 minutes to get where I'm going? Then I'll leave 17 minutes before I need to be there.

And that was a nightmare. I seemed to always be stressed. I was worried I was going to be late. Then I'd be late. That would make me feel awful, which carried into whatever meeting I was showing up to.

Now I build a ridiculous cushion into my estimates of how long it will take me to get somewhere. If I have to be at the airport two hours early, I'll plan on getting there three hours early. That way, if there's an unexpected traffic jam, I have time for it. If I get there with three hours to spare, I can now spend that time at the gate working on emails, writing this book, or some other productive use of time. The other way to do it is just too costly. If I spend those hours at home working on emails, and then miss my flight, I've let down my client, damaged my reputation, and missed out on a paycheck. Not having that cushion is literally too expensive in terms of time, money, and reputation not to have.

So in your daily life, assume things will take longer to accomplish than you think they will, and plan your day accordingly. That way, if it gets done sooner, you can start on your next task even earlier. At the end of the day you might have some time left over that you can spend on those things you "never have time for." You'll be amazed how much you wind up accomplishing with this approach.

This is completely backwards from how most people try to get stuff done. Most people are how I used to be; trying to schedule everything out to the exact minute.

The problem happens when things start to overlap. Now you have colliding obligations and traffic jams of duties. This winds up eating up more time than you're saving, and you're constantly behind schedule. By planning on doing less, you'll have more time to get more done.

Notice I'm not saying that you have to be doing work from the moment you wake up until the moment you go to sleep. People who never take time away from their jobs are like people who only breathe out. Do that long enough and you'll pass out! So if you don't make time to take care of yourself upfront, you'll eventually have to take time for being sick. Better to do it on your terms instead of having it imposed on you without warning.

Don't cut corners. Don't cheat your duties. Don't spend forever on any one thing. Create the amount of time you need for something, get it done, and move on to the next thing. Organize the time you create, and use it to the best of your abilities. Make time for effort. Make time for rest. Ignore either at your own peril. Soon you'll find that the more productive you become, the more time you'll have for relaxing.

This is how you protect the time you create from the twin thieves of indecision and procrastination. Cushions will protect you from scheduling traffic jams (literal and figurative), and organizing will save your sanity. Stop wasting time thinking about could and would and focus instead on what you can and will. Past mistakes aren't worth your time either. The best way to stop worrying about them is to learn what they have to teach you, and apply those lessons to future decisions. Spending any more time than that is time wasted.

Exponential Time

Something we absolutely must talk about is the effect time has on our choices. Time doesn't just add to a choice; time multiplies it.

The sooner you make a decision, the more time there is for its effect to play out. The more time it's in effect, the more effect it can have in the future. Time compounds the effect, making it a recursive multiplier. The more you do with the time you have, the more time you'll have to do what you want. If you've ever heard of compounded interest, you'll recognize this principle.

There's a word problem I ran across a while ago that illustrates the point. It says, "If a chessboard were to have a grain of rice placed on each square such that one grain were placed on the first square, two on the second, four on the third, and so on (doubling the number of grains on each subsequent square), how many grains of rice would be on the chessboard by the 64th square?"

The answer is 18,446,744,073,709,551,615 grain of rice! That's a number much higher than I expected when I first did the math. But that's not where we stop. In terms of the question, we only dealt with double the previous number. Here's what happens when we add the accumulation of time.

On Day 1 we have 1 grain of rice. The next day, on Day 2, we double that number which gives us 2; but we now add the single grain we still have from Day 1. We now have 3 grains total. Then on Day 3 we double that, which gives us 6 new grains of rice. Add the 6 new grains to the 3 grains we already have, for a total of 9 grains on Day 3. If you carry this process out 64 times you'll get a total of 1,144,561,273,430,837,49 4,885,949,696,427 grains of rice! To give you an idea of how much rice that is, it weighs the same amount as five Earths.

That's exactly what happens with the effects of your choices over time. You wind up adding to the original effect every day. You have the results of what you've done yesterday to work with today. It's basically daily compounded interest on your effort. When you put in a little bit every day, it winds up making a massive difference! The problem is, most people don't understand this principle, so they change direction before they start to notice results. But you absolutely must put in daily effort to maintain momentum. Otherwise you have to start all over at the beginning at zero.

Jonathan **Pritchard**

Chapter 8: The Lens of Your Mind

On a bright day the amount of sunlight that falls on six square inches of Earth can start a fire, if you know how to focus it with a magnifying lens. If the lens is held too far away, nothing happens. If the lens is dirty, nothing happens. If the tinder is wet, nothing happens. Only when all the elements are combined just right can you concentrate the power of the sun to create fire.

Same goes for your thinking. If it is clear, then you can make the most out of your mental energy. You can cut straight to the heart of a problem without wasting energy on useless thought patterns. This is the power of concentration. Concentration is the ability to focus your thinking on a single idea, and to keep it there. Easier said than done!

Try an experiment that my high school debate teacher Bob Yutzy had us do once in class. Set a timer for two minutes, and then try to think of only one thing. Choose an object near you. Maybe a mug, a pencil, key, or doorknob. For the next two minutes, focus solely on that object. Allow no other thought to enter your mind, no matter what. Your whole world is that object. The instant anything other than that object enters your mind, you must admit defeat. Give it a go; this book will still be here when you come back.

How was it? Tougher than you expected, right? Before you know it your mind is playing a free-association game, and you're eleven million miles away in three seconds flat! This phenomenon is well-known to anyone who meditates, and is called "Monkey Mind." That's the term to describe an untrained mind that is unsettled, restless, capricious, whimsical, fanciful, inconstant, confused, indecisive, and uncontrollable. Sound familiar? Sure does to me!

Here's another exercise to see how well you can concentrate. Try counting to five. That's it. Count to five without allowing a thought of anything else to enter your mind. The only thing you can allow is the act of counting. This is more abstract than concentrating on the object because you're not actually focusing on reality; the numbers are solely in your mind. This actually makes it more difficult. Try it, and if you're being honest with yourself (good luck with that!), then you'll probably have to admit you can't do it the first time. The instant a different thought intrudes, start over. Maybe a bird chirps and your mind goes to that. Start over. Maybe a car drives past and you listen to that. Start over. Stick to it long enough and you might get all the way up to ten. Maybe.

Why am I making such a fuss over something that

seems so simple? The object exercise and counting are simply there to illustrate a point: the ability to keep your mind where you want it is like being able to focus the power of a thousand suns.

Here's a real-life example: You're about to leave your apartment on your way to work, and there's a problem you want to solve before you get there. You lock the door, go down the elevator, and you've gone less than half a block before what? That's right! Your mind has wandered over a hundred topics that aren't the problem. None of them are important either, are they? On it continues until you get to the office, and you arrive without a solution in hand. Sure, you'll get to it eventually; but the point is that had you been able to keep your mind where you want it, it would have saved you significant amounts of time, the most important resource! How much time have you wasted in the past hour thinking about useless things? In the past day? Week? Month? Year? Add to that all the compounded interest you're missing. Now you see that it's a problem of astronomical importance!

It goes farther, too. You actually don't currently know what most of your problems are. You've never thought about it properly before! It's like there's a mental fog that clouds your thinking. This lets your problems lurk in the shadows, where they sometimes stay hidden for years. You're only aware of them as some vague ominous presence never quite taking definite shape. They wear down our mental efforts until we're exhausted from being tense, uncomfortable, and anxious all the time.

Concentration will keep you from doing too little everywhere and focus all that you have on a single area. This will burn away the fog, and reveal the heart of the matter to you. Once you see the actual problem clearly, you can take the appropriate actions to solve it once and for all. To help you do this, find a pen and a piece of paper. Don't do this on a computer; this needs to be a physical experience where you see your hand making a mark in reality. Take the pen and write down a problem you've had for awhile. You might realize it's difficult to put down in words because it's vague in your mind. You might find yourself writing down symptoms of the problem instead of naming the problem, proper. It's just like Thoreau said: "For every thousand hacking at the leaves of evil, there is one striking at the root." We could say, "For every thousand thoughts you have about a problem, there is one striking at the root." Maybe you're anticipating what might happen. Maybe you're considering things that don't affect the outcome at all. None of that matters, and it should not concern you. Get through all those to eventually uncover the crux of the matter in all its naked glory.

You'll realize that by focusing only on the problem, you've gotten to see its real shape. Now that you've gotten rid of its cloud of confusion, you can do something about it. Since you know what is actually wrong, your efforts to fix it will be 100 percent focused on solving it. Make a list of everything that's in your way of accomplishing that. Really write it out. Before you know it, you'll have a clear path to freedom that you've never thought possible. This is the process of defining your problem and then organizing your thoughts to solve it. That's the lion's share of the hard work, and you haven't even done anything yet! Do this process with everything that's bothering you, and you'll amaze yourself at how quickly you fix problems you've been tinkering with for years. You're going to have to find a new hobby because "worry about problems" won't work for you anymore.

My life's prayer is to have more interesting problems. You're never going to get rid of having problems. You can, however, get rid of the ones you currently have to make way for more interesting ones you can't even imagine having right now. It's the ability to concentrate that makes all the difference in the world. You'll soon be taking action in a smart and direct way that will get you results faster than you ever dreamed possible.

Chapter 9: Emerging Framework for Environmental Governance

Earlier I mentioned getting to work with James Randi, which was a pleasure because he also hosted a science conference every year in Las Vegas called "The Amaz!ng Meeting." Every year for thirteen years I was involved in some way. Either I helped at registration, worked on filling out the schedule, and a couple years I even performed for a room full of 1,500 science enthusiasts!

One of the highlights of my time working with the Amaz!ng Meeting was getting to meet notable scientists like Neil deGrasse Tyson, Bill Nye, and Ed Lu the American astronaut who I helped float magically on stage! During a panel with Neil deGrasse Tyson, Bill Nye, Pamela Gay, and Lawrence Krauss about the future of space travel, Neil said something interesting. He argued that the future of humankind can only be as a spacefaring peoples, and as such the governments of the world should put many more resources into funding space exploration.

He continued to essentially say that taxes have historically paid for the spread of human civilization before privatized ventures recognize the value and swoop in to make things cheaper, faster, and easier. Columbus sailing the Atlantic? A government backed adventure. Sacagawea, Lewis, and Clark? Government backed adventure. Human beings landing on the moon (and coming back home)? Government adventure.

In each case, private entities came through after the governmental investment paid off. Now, are we going to keep talking about how tax dollars are used? Of course not! Why am I talking about taxes, then? I chose a topic that was 1) boring as all get-out, and 2) took a stance that most people might not be happy with, so that 3) they would skip this chapter.

Why?

I'm going to teach you a mind reading trick! We've had enough theory, doom-'n-gloom, and general ideas already. I want to reward you for sticking with me this far, so now you get to learn the fun stuff. You're going to see how to use this book to convince your friends, the person sitting next to you on the plane, or Steve in Accounting to think you can read their minds. And it's easy. All the hard work is already done for you.

Effect: You flip through the book and the spectator tells you when to stop. You ask them to remember the last word on the top line, and tell you when they've done this. Once they're ready you close the book, set it aside, stare into their eyes, and reveal the word they are merely thinking of. Nothing is written, no questions are asked, and no setup is necessary. Starting a cult is optional.

Method: This book is gimmicked! Maybe you've already noticed the secret, but didn't know you were looking at a magic trick. This is the essence of magic: hide the secret in plain sight. Check out the title at the top of the previous page. The word inside the bracket is different for every page, and that's for a very specific reason: it tells you what the last word of the top line on the opposite page. Here's how this helps you.

Hold the book by the spine in your right hand. With your left hand at the top corner flip through the pages. From your perspective you should be able to see the word inside the brackets quite easily. Note: If there's no word in the bracket, the opposite page is blank!

Performance: When your friend asks you what you're reading, tell them, "Oh, it's a book on how to think like a mind reader. I think I'm getting the hang of it. Want to try it out?" When they say yes, hold the book by the spine with your right hand and the cover facing them. This will make sure the open side of the pages is pointing to your left. Then say, "I'm going to flip through the pages like this, and when you say 'stop' I'll stop. Just like that." Demonstrate your actions as you explain, and then do it for real. When they say stop, say, "Can you see the last word on the top line there? Don't worry about any chapter titles, or anything. Just the top sentence," tapping the area with your left fingers to indicate where they should be looking. This is your chance to look down at the page you can see which will tell you what word they can see. Do this quickly and easily, but not so fast as to appear like you're trying to hide something. It's more like you're directing them where to look with your eyes, and you naturally glance at the book for a moment before returning your attention to them. Once you know what the word is, turn your head away like you don't want to be accused of peeking, and keep your face turned away until the book is closed and placed on the table.

Now the rest is pure theatrics. It's interesting to note: For your friend the trick hasn't even really started, but for you, the hard part is already done. This is the essence of thinking like a mind reader; get so far ahead of the person you're dealing with that they can never hope to catch up! It's all about preparation, confidence, communication, and managing their attention.

There are plenty of ways to reveal the word they're thinking of, but the one you want to avoid is just blurting it out. That makes the whole thing a puzzle for them to figure out. What you want to do is give their mind some sort of plausible explanation for how you're able to know what they're thinking of. This is a sort of "red herring," and it's absolutely critical for the success of the trick. As you know, we humans work on assumptions about how the world works, and one of the big ones is that if you're doing something strange, it must be important. Ever thought about why a magician waves a wand and says magic words? Your "logic mind" knows it's all showmanship, but the deeper reptile brain buys the charade hook-line-and-sinker. You're going to do the same to your friend.

Ask your friend to imagine like they're about to say the word, but not to actually say it out loud. Tell them to imagine catching it in their mouth, and then pantomime blowing a soap bubble. Encourage them to blow through it. Say, "Now your word is trapped in that imaginary soap bubble! Can you see it?!" Encourage them to play along by nodding your head. Reach out with one hand and mime popping the bubble with your other hand underneath, ready to catch the word as it drops out. Look down at your hand that holds the word, and "read" it out loud as though you're unsure it's correct. Your friend will be stunned.

Really visualize these things happening. This is absolutely imperative. You need to believe in your magic before anyone else can. Forget that this doesn't make one bit of logical sense in reality. Allow yourself to buy into the power of your imagination, and your friend will follow you. What you're doing through your actions is providing their brain with what I like to call "Cartoon Logic."

Have you watched any Wile E. Coyote cartoons? For some reason it makes sense that he runs off a cliff, but doesn't fall until he looks down. That's not how physics works in the real world, but in the world of Wile E. Coyote, it is. The same goes for your demonstrations of mental powers. In the real world nobody can really read minds, but in your world you can know the word someone's thinking about if they blow an imaginary bubble with the word inside. Its logic is internally consistent, and that's what makes it so powerful. It makes no real sense, but it will feel like a real answer to your friend even though they won't think about it consciously. Your words and actions are speaking directly to their subconscious by bypassing the conscious mind completely. Their conscious mind is too busy thinking "This is silly" while their subconscious says "This feels right!"

Now you can see why I've waited this long to include this chapter. I needed you to understand just how deep your mind goes, and to know how much is going on under the surface without you knowing about it. This is how your life plays out. Others can't believe in you until you do first. You can never accept more love than you allow yourself to feel first. Everyone you meet will respond to these fundamental subconscious beliefs you carry with you everywhere you go. That's why every time you try to run from your problems, they show up again. You've done nothing to address the fundamental beliefs that govern how you choose to interact with the world. You control the magic in your life. Now you can see it.

I hope you perform this trick for many different people, and give them a glimpse into a world where anything is possible. Hopefully this will give you the confidence to make the magic come alive in your own life as well. Let it be a reminder to you every time you perform it. The best way to create magic in your own life is to help others see it in theirs (as I hope I've done for you).

Chapter 10: The True Names of Your Demons

For as long as I can remember I've loved ancient Egypt. It's full of interesting facts and surprises. For example: Cleopatra lived sooner to the building of the first Pizza Hut than to the building of the Great Pyramids. See? Egypt is still full of surprises!

Back then, written languages were still a relatively new technology. Today we take for granted how powerful language actually is. It's one of the first creations of abstract reasoning. Spoken language allows you to know something, make some sounds, and suddenly teach someone else what you know. The problem is, it's a very ephemeral experience; if you're not in that particular place at that particular time, you'll never know what was communicated. That's where written language comes in. Written language allows you to encode your ideas into symbols that are stored within some medium like clay tablets, stones, or paper. Hundreds or thousands of years can go by, and someone can look at those symbols and have the same thought as the author had long ago. That's powerful magic!

It's such powerful magic that Egyptians thought if you knew the true name of something, you would have power over it. This is why they had several names for the same person. And, in a way, they were 100 percent right. Imagine you hear a sound at night. You have no clue what is making it, but it's freaking you out. As long as you don't know its source, it will continue to bother you. The instant you identify it as a branch on your window, you can relax. You've "named the problem."

This is applicable to the performing arena. Back when I was getting my start working open mic nights at bars, I would have people recognize me as the mind reader and tell me, "Oh you should use my friend Bill over there! He's a ham, so he'd be perfect for your tricks!" The problem is, natural hams often make the worst volunteers, because all they know how to do is be the center of attention at any cost. They don't know how to manage a fun experience for a room full of people! They also happen to be ideal candidates for becoming a heckler. I'd get halfway through my performance when Bill would decide this is his opportunity to chime in without an invite. He'd shout something to interrupt the show, but if I ignored it, the interruptions would only get worse.

Here's what I would do. I would thank my volunteer onstage for being patient with me as I take care of this, and then turn towards Bill. I'd then say something along the lines of, "Sir, I appreciate your interest in the show, but you're interrupting the fun of sixty people for something that can wait. If you really want to be involved, I can pick you for something later, Bill, I promise."

This did several things. It lets the audience know I'm not going to allow the performance to be derailed completely by knuckleheads. It gives Bill some attention so he feels heard. And it scares him. "How did he know my name?!" he thinks. It's unnerving to have someone know who you are, but have no clue who they are.

That's why I touched on this in Chapter 8. You absolutely must be able to see to the heart of a problem to see its root, not just the branches it creates. Most folks are concerned with the symptoms of their problem instead of the fundamental cause of it.

Most of your big problems are created from a host of smaller ones coming together in a way that overwhelms you. No matter how big or small they are, you must be able to face them. Plus, it's often the small-time problems that keep us from dealing with the big issues. Maybe we don't even know the difference between the two! My advice, then, is to deal with what's on your mind right now. What's the problem that's been eating at the edges of your mind? What's been taking up precious brain power? Your mind can only consider one problem at a time, so go ahead and deal with what's in front of you right now.

Don't be surprised, however, to find another problem ready to take the spot of the one you just fixed. Such is life; there's always going to be problems, but this way you'll make more progress than you would have otherwise.

This principle of "one at a time" applies across the board. Instead of getting overwhelmed by how much you have left to do, focus instead on what you can do right now. Take a moment to appreciate the enormity of the situation as a whole, sure, but then commit to taking one step at a time no matter how small. This is the only way to make progress. The longer you delay, the longer your problem will have to haunt you. The longer it haunts you, the more difficult it will be to exorcise it. The three ghosts who will visit most often are uncertainty, doubt, and indecision. Instead of letting them erode your sanity, name them to strip them of their power, then dispel them by taking action. As the incredible painter Vincent Van Gogh said about uncertainty and doubt, "If you hear a voice within you say 'you cannot paint,' then by all means paint, and that voice will be silenced."

Boss Level Demons

But what about the really big problems like being broke? Or lonely? Or being sick all the time? Surely these aren't my fault, are they?

No. I'm not going to victim blame. What I am going to do is strongly encourage you to take ownership of what you can do about something rather than lament what you can't do about it. Many people try to make themselves feel better about a situation by reminding themselves that there's always someone worse off than them. I know I have. "At least I'm not homeless," I'd think. Then I was homeless for awhile. The problem is, thinking about how someone else has it worse than you doesn't do any good about your situation! It does absolutely nothing to solve your problem; it's temporary relief from a symptom at best. At worst it makes things deteriorate even more because it's had more time to affect you!

The absolute rock-bottom truth you must accept is that the only person obligated to take care of you is you. For years I believed that my sagging career was the fault of agents who weren't holding up their end of the bargain by not booking me enough. It wasn't until I understood that I was neglecting to work on my own business that things started to improve. I blamed everyone but the person responsible for my money woes; me!

If you're short on money, like every single person I meet it seems, then there are really only two solutions. First is make more money. Easier said than done, right? "Fat lot of good that does me in this economy," you could say. You would if you could already, right?

Maybe. Maybe not. There are plenty of reasons why people don't make as much as they'd like. Maybe they just don't want to work hard. Maybe they're willing to work harder than anyone else, but aren't willing to change location. Maybe they're plain scared of change. Maybe they lack the confidence in their abilities.

I can tell you, though, I've seen more times than I can count people who stay in the same place, doing the same things year after year, who tell themselves there aren't any opportunities. Let me tell you the hard truth. Opportunity doesn't find you. You make opportunities happen. You create them. Opportunity is a way of thinking combined with taking appropriate action. Spend the time you usually reserve to lamenting a situation on solving it, and you'll be surprised what you can achieve.

The other way to have more money is to manage what you already have. I often remind myself of an idea I heard a long time ago: "That which gets measured, gets managed." When was the last time you accounted for your spending? Have you actually tallied up how much you're spending on the different areas of your life? You might be surprised how much is going towards purchases that aren't actively improving your quality of life.

Now I'm not saying there aren't situations and systems outside your control that impact your life. What I am saying, though, is you'll do more good for yourself and those in your life the instant you focus on what you can do about the problem instead of what you can't do.

Own Your Demons or They Will Own You

Continually ask yourself whether you're putting effort towards finding a solution, or into perpetuating the problem. In many more cases than you might be willing to admit, you are the problem. Out of all the problems in your life, remember, you're the only common denominator.

Now, health concerns are quite often way outside your control. We don't get to pick our parents, nor the genetic poker hand we were dealt. But if you were being honest with yourself, when was the last time you did something to improve your health? How often do you reward yourself with a little treat because "you earned it?" We all suffer, but we often get to choose what kind we experience. You can choose to suffer the pain of discipline, or the pain of regret when it's too late to do anything about it.

What Counts Most

You know what I care about? I don't care one bit about what you can't do. I care about what you can do!

That's the only thing that can ever get anything done. "Can't" never built a single thing in the whole history of human existence. If you have some sort of disability, I'm not going to tell you that someone else is worse off. I don't care. What I am going to say is that you're capable of something. And the instant you focus on what you can do, you've decided to take responsibility and ownership for your own happiness. Your attitude is more important than your aptitude. It's the mind that sets you free, or keeps you a captive. There are those who go through terrible experiences who come out the other side more capable and resilient for it, while there are people living lives of luxury who are absolutely miserable with it.

Don't you dare tell me I can't do something. Show me what I can do. Look to Helen Keller who had every excuse to live a miserable life; and she was on track to do exactly that until someone believed in her, and showed her what she could do. By focusing on how she could communicate with the world instead of all the ways she couldn't, she was able to live a life of inspiration and accomplishment. The instant you tell someone there's nothing to be done is the instant you've relegated them to a life of misery and pain. I choose to inspire and encourage, thank you very much. As one of my best friends and source of personal inspiration David Hira says, "Be a faucet, not a drain."

Chapter 11: Repeat As Necessary

"You are what you do repeatedly, so your excellence isn't an act, it's a habit," said writer and philosopher Will Durant in 1926.

Farther back in history Greek playwright Archilochus said, "We don't rise to the level of our expectations, we fall to the level of our training."

Both men are talking about the same thing: the indisputable power that habit has to shape our lives. We aren't living according to a few moments that shape our destiny; it is instead the consistent effort we put in day after day which dictates the course we take.

What percentage of your choices would you think are the result of habit instead of rational decisionmaking? Five percent? Ten? As high as 25?

Turns out it's more like 40 to 45 percent of your actions, ones that feel like the result of choices we consciously make, are actually the result of ingrained patterns of behavior we like to call habits. Nearly half the actions you take are the result of autopilot! That's staggering to me, but it makes sense when you think about it. What's the first thing you do when you wake up? Do you take a few moments to enjoy the process of slowly coming back to reality, or are you unlocking your phone to check emails and Facebook?

You're not awake yet and you're already letting other people tell you what you should be thinking! I don't like doing that. My mornings at home usually looks like this: wake up around 6:30 am without an alarm. I immediately get out of bed and do my kung fu forms. (Think yoga, but with more punching and kicking.) If it's a Monday, Wednesday, or Friday I follow kung fu with an hour and a half of stretching and a bodyweight workout before making coffee from beans grown on a small organic farm in Costa Rica run by an American couple who retired there. Only after I've had a couple hours to my own mind do I even think about opening the computer, and I still don't open Facebook or email. That can still wait. I spend at least a half hour working on my business by reaching out to clients, looking for folks to connect with on LinkedIn, or writing an article on the website. Only after I've done the stuff I need to do to keep myself mentally, physically, emotionally, and wholistically healthy, do I then engage with the outside world.

This wasn't always my morning. I wasn't in the habit. I used to wake up, roll over, check Facebook, send some texts, etc. But it can be changed. Before we get into how to do that, however, let's look at why we do what we do. What's our motivation?

Everything I Learned About Motivation, I Learned From an Amoeba

A single-celled organism might seem like a strange place to look for understanding human decisions, but we're less different than you might think. Amoebas have no central nervous system, no brain, nor memory, but they do have rudimentary chemical receptors which function as a sort of sense of smell. If you put sulfuric acid into an amoeba's environment, it will "smell" the danger, and move away from what will bring it lots of pain. On the other hand, if you put a small piece of algae, bacteria, or plant matter that amoebas love to eat nearby, its sense of smell will tell it to move towards the food. This is the secret to all motivation. Living creatures move towards pleasure, and away from pain. That includes you.

"But Jonathan," you think, "I'm much more complex than an amoeba, and I can think of a zillion ways your comparison doesn't hold up. For example, I smoke, which I know is bad for me, and I don't go to the gym which I know is good for me. Explain that, Mr. Mind Reader Man!"

Happy to oblige. You're still operating on the very basic level of pain and pleasure. Smoking feels good now. You get to spend some time outside in the sunlight, you get to take a break from your desk, and you might even meet some other cool people on the patio as you share a light. These are all pleasant experiences. Not to mention the little buzz you get from the nicotine! In the here and now, which is the only time that matters, smoking feels good. Who cares about the distant future where you may, or may not, get emphysema. Why don't you go to the gym? Because it hurts! Sitting on the couch now feels so much better than lifting weights, running six miles, or doing the Stairmaster. Cardio is monotonous and boring. How much better is it to sit here and zone out while we binge another season on Netflix?! See? You're a human-sized amoeba.

But things do get more complicated. Ever heard of Pavlov, the father of understanding conditioned responses? His name might "ring a bell." He was a Russian psychologist who was studying salivation in dogs at feeding time. This is a natural reaction that is hardwired into dogs (and even humans). It isn't learned, it's genetically programmed into the dog. Pavlov noticed that before long the dogs started salivating when he walked into the room, even when he wasn't carrying food. It didn't take him long to realize that the dogs had learned to associate his presence with the presence of food, so his presence alone would trigger the ingrained salivation response. He then experimented with ringing a bell as he fed the dogs. Sure enough, before long he could ring the bell without food present, yet the dogs would still start drooling. They had learned to associate feeding time with the sound of the bell. This is the essence of classical conditioning.

It's important to note that this kind of conditioning can happen very quickly, and I use it in my walkaround performances. Companies will bring me in during their event's cocktail hour to help people mingle. If I'm not there to break the ice and connect people who may not otherwise talk with each other, they'll get bored and withdraw. With me, however, people from different departments have a shared experience to chat about, and nothing brings people together faster than shared laughter. This is where classic conditioning comes in handy. I introduce myself to a small group of people and perform my first routine, which gets them interested in knowing more. It's lighthearted and funny, which is a great tone to set at the beginning. When the person on either side of me laughs, I'll reinforce it by lightly touching them on the shoulder as I say, "Right?!" and nod my head. The second time they laugh I do exactly the same thing. Touch their shoulder while saying, "Right?!" and nod my head. Now, if I want them to laugh as something that's not even funny, I can do it in the same tone of voice, touch them on the should, say, "Right?!" and nod my head. What do you think happens? They laugh! The touch on the shoulder is "anchored" to the physiological experience of laughing. They've been conditioned to do it, subconsciously. This sounds like evil voodoo, but the good news is, conditioning that happens that quickly will fade just as fast. I couldn't come back a year later and get the same response with just the physical anchor. But, it's important to note that they will still associate me with how happy they felt when they were around me. Or as Carl W. Buehner put it, "They may forget what you said — but they will never forget how you made them feel."

Classical conditioning, and how it makes you feel, is the explanation for why you engage in behaviors that hurt you long-term, and avoid behaviors that help you long-term. You've learned to associate the positive behaviors as being painful, and the harmful behaviors as being pleasurable. You're conditioned to behave that way by an intricate system of triggers, behaviors, and rewards. You're moving away from what you've learned to think will be painful, and you're moving towards what you've learned to think will be pleasurable. These pain/pleasure associations are created without your conscious involvement or awareness, yet they subconsciously govern nearly half your daily choices.

That Adds Up

All the fractions of your life add up to 1. That's why you can never remove a bad habit; you can only replace it with a better habit. So let's look at how habits are formed subconsciously, so we can consciously build better habits later.

Habits consist of three parts. First is the cue. There's some person, item, sound, time of day, or touch that triggers the pattern of behavior. That behavior (or behaviors, plural) are the conditioned response. This is the autopilot part of the sequence. Then there's the reward. What are you getting out of doing this? That's why in dog training, you always ask yourself, "Where's the value in the dog behaving like this?" There's always a reward, and that's what signals the brain that "hey, if we want [reward] we get it by [behavior] when I see [cue]."

Most people focus solely on changing their behavior, but that's only a third of the equation, and one of the less important parts at that. What really can make a permanent change is digging into your triggers and rewards.

When we engage in a new behavior, we usually have to give it some conscious thought. That happens in the prefrontal cortex which is where most of our conscious processes live, a relatively recent section of the brain from an evolutionary standpoint. Pretty quickly, though, you need to give less and less attention to the behavior, because it's being encoded in a deeper part of your brain called the basal ganglia, which is part of your subconscious processes. That's why you can be in the middle of doing something before you're even conscious you're doing it; it's not a conscious choice at that point! This is why consciously deciding to change your habits doesn't work too well; that's not where they live! It's like consciously deciding to see the Eiffel Tower in Iowa.

If you want to change a pattern of behavior, the best way to go about it is to identify its cue and reward. What's the trigger, and what's the payoff? There are usually five elements that influence our behaviors: they can be a person, place, time, emotion, or ritual (which is kind of a combination of the other four triggers). Now you get to play Sherlock Holmes. Every time you find yourself in the middle of the old habit, write down a detail about each of those five elements. Who is present? Where are you? What time of day is it? How are you feeling? What were you doing right before this? The act of writing it down pulls you out of autopilot, and brings to the forefront what's usually going on under the surface. Also, if you actually take the time to write it all down in one place, and are consistent with it, you'll quickly find the common denominator between each craving or habit. Now you get to figure out the most important part; what are you getting out of it?

Habits are never about the behavior itself; it's always about what you're getting out of it, and that can be surprisingly difficult to pinpoint. Habits are a complex cocktail of physical, mental, emotional, intellectual, and social motivations. We have a multitude of explanations for why we do things; but as Anthony

Robbins figured out from Maslow's Hierarchy of Needs, everything we do in our lives boils down to the need to feel certainty, variety, connection, growth, significance, and/or contribution. The more of these needs a single behavior includes, the more powerful the desire to perform the habit becomes.

That's why when I feel a craving for a brownie, I'm not just looking for something sweet. If that were true, chewing gum would fit the bill. Instead I'm looking for that same sense of connection I felt with my mom when we made brownies together when I was young. I felt certain when we baked together that we were going to have a good time. I felt significant because she was making the effort to spend time just with me, and I was contributing to the experience by helping with the baking. That's four out of six needs right there! No wonder I'd turn to brownies if I felt like I was missing out on any of those emotions.

You'll have to do a bit more sleuthing on your own to figure out which of those needs your habit is checking off for you. But now that you know the structure of how habits function, it will be much easier to work your way out of it. Once you bring to light these subconscious mental routines of cue, habit, and reward, you can consciously plan new behaviors that can meet the same needs as the old behavior without the negative collateral damage. You now choose the new set of behaviors by "future pacing." This is imagining yourself in a future situation where you're presented with the same cue, choosing to engage in a new sequence of behaviors, to achieve the reward(s) you're looking for. It won't be easy at first. In fact, it will be quite difficult to prevent the old pattern from playing out. But with practice and consistent effort, you'll overwrite the old habit with the new, more effective habit. After a couple months, you'll find yourself in the middle of the new habit without even being aware you're doing it!

Hopefully you see now why sheer willpower alone doesn't work. And now you also hopefully understand why some people seem to play "bad habit merry-go-round." They stop smoking, and start biting their nails. They stop biting their nails, and start shoplifting. They never take the time to unpack the unexpressed needs those behaviors are fulfilling, so the fundamental issue is never addressed; it's just how it's expressed that changes shape!

Move the World

You may understand the cue > behavior > reward cycle, and still not make the change you're looking for. Sometimes, if a habit is particularly difficult to replace, you need the big gun: leverage. "Give me a lever long enough and a fulcrum on which to place it, and I shall move the world." Archimedes knew what he was talking about. Sometimes, you just don't care.

You know all the facts. You know you should make a change. But you still couldn't care less. The problem is, you haven't found that thing that you care enough about, that would demand you changing to get. Fortunately for you, I know how your brain works, and I'm about to give you the secret.

We're loss aversion creatures. That is to say, we've evolved to care more about keeping what we already have than what we could possibly gain by giving it up (even if it's orders of magnitude better). We're scared of losing more than we're excited by gaining. Weird, right? There are plenty of folk sayings along this vein: "The devil we know is better than the one we don't," "One bird in the hand is better than two in the bush," etc. So how do you use it to your benefit? Exactly by embracing it. Don't focus on what you could gain, but at what you could lose.

Want to do pushups? Don't think about how big your arms are going to get. Tell a friend of yours, "Hey, for the next week I'm going to try doing twenty pushups a day. Every time I miss a day, I'm going to give you twenty bucks." Now, what do you think you'll be focused on?! Making sure you're not going to lose your twenty dollars today! There's even online technology built to help you with this. Behavioral economists at Yale, who study this kind of thing, set up a platform over at stickk.com. Set your goal, intended behavior, or outcome; define the stakes at $10, $20, $100, etc;

and then designate a referee who will evaluate your success or failure. It's that simple. This keeps you accountable, provides negative reinforcement for not following through, and will get you taking action faster than just hoping, wishing, or praying about it! It works.

Hopefully now you have a better handle on why you do what you do, what you get out of doing it, and how to use this knowledge to make more conscious decisions about how to spend your time.

Chapter 12: Follow Your [   ]!

What word would you put in those brackets? Most self-help gurus would tell you to follow your passion, and that's quite possibly the worst advice I've ever heard. Don't you think if you already had a passion, you wouldn't need some blissed-out weirdo telling you to find it? But chances are you don't have a passion. Or you do, but every couple of years your passion changes as you continue to "find yourself." (Another equally useless platitude, if you ask me. You're reading this book, so you are!) Following your passion is a great excuse for ruining your life.

Now, don't get me wrong. There are people who pursue what they're passionate about, and they make it big. And that's my point. You typically only see the people who made it onto Oprah, who are there as a cheerleader for you to quit your job, be a yoga instructor, and follow your inner light. The problem is, you don't see the thousands and thousands of other people who quit their good paying job, and went through 200 hours of yogi training for thousands of dollars, just to graduate with no understanding of how to build a client network, no experience with running their own business, nor any other skills required to work for themselves. But, hey! They have lots of passion! Cut to three years later, and they're broke, back to their old job, three years' lost seniority, and a whole heap of resentment for something they used to love.

Let me tell you about how I ruined my life by following my passion to the exclusion of all else. When I was five years old I saw a magician on The Tonight Show and I knew what I wanted to do with my life. I read every book I could get my hands on, my parents got me a magic trick for every birthday, and over time I figured out I love the mind-reading tricks the most. Every single choice I've made since I was five has been filtered by this single question: How does this help get me closer to being a professional mentalist? It was the perfect context for me to explore my creativity. Everything I could be interested in could be expressed in some way in my business.

And I sacrificed everything. Being around my family. A marriage. The list of things I've given up in exchange for following my passion is everything I could point to. Like I said in the introduction, I'd traveled the world, entertained overseas troops, performed on Vegas main stages, and partied hard. But I rarely saw my friends. I lived in hotels and saw the inside of rental cars more than my own apartment. I couldn't even keep a plant alive. But my identity was completely wrapped up in "I'm a professional performer!" and I couldn't imagine doing anything else with my time. And, that's what was slowly killing my happiness. I had gotten what I wanted, but the price was too high.

People are searching for their all-consuming passion; that thing that gets them fired up. The problem is, that fire usually burns everything to a crisp! Their sense of purpose, identity, and self is wrapped up in "finding their passion." If that's you, I'm here to let you off the hook. Don't worry about it. Why? If you were going to have a passion, don't you think you'd have found it already? Also, don't you think you'd know you'd found it? All this talk about how to find your passion doesn't help anybody! So, what works?

Curiosity

There are two ways to go through life: as though everything is a miracle, or as if nothing is a miracle. I choose the first! I can never wrap my head around people who discover something completely unknown to them and completely ignore it. How do they do that?! They rarely ask "how" or "why" about anything. They're only interested in the "what."

One of our most useful tools as well-adjusted human beings is our sense of curiosity. Every single advancement in the history of humans was the result of someone being curious about something, and digging into it. You're probably familiar with the first half of the saying, "Curiosity killed the cat," which is typically bandied about as a warning by those who are scared of venturing outside the boundary of convention. But have you ever heard the rest of the saying? It's, "...

and satisfaction brought him back." Almost nobody knows that! The satisfaction of following your curiosity will kill nothing but your ignorance. The more you know about the world, and how it works, the better equipped you'll be to make better choices.

Too many people walk through life with their head down, eyes forward, and zero interest about the million wonderful things they pass every single day. Their attention is focused only on their problems, thoughts, and frustrations. I'd be completely surprised if anyone with that disposition discovered a major breakthrough in the human experience!

The people you hear about are the people who are intensely curious about the world. I've mentioned Elon Musk already. He's one curious guy! He doesn't take anything for granted. He asks why, why not, and how can we about things you and I think are already settled. As a result, he's created the world's first reusable rocket. It's a huge leap forward for humanity as a whole, and we have his curiosity to thank for it. If Einstein hadn't been curious about the nature of space and time, we may never have created GPS satellites that can account for the warpage of time at high velocities which allow you to reach your destination with a device in your pocket.

Curiosity and interested are two sides to the same coin. You can't have one without the other. People who aren't interested in anything rarely have curiosity. If you don't have curiosity about anything, you're probably not interested in it, either. If you lack one, or both, you're probably familiar with their arch nemesis: boredom. I'm a huge believer that only boring people are bored. The flip side is also true: interested people are interesting! The only way to cure boredom is to discover something new about the world that you didn't know before. Get interested about something!

Maybe you're not bored yet, but you're on the track. There's a dangerous middle ground where you consistently shy away from anything that might present a challenge to you, your way of thinking, or your abilities. You never challenge yourself. You never get familiar with the experience of being uncomfortable. You prefer the tried-and-true approach to anything. There are plenty of people who think anything that can be discovered has been discovered. These are the folks who think nothing is a miracle. They can watch me reveal the most intimate secrets of a perfect stranger, see them freak out, and think, "Oh, they're probably an actor who he pays to play along" before turning to the next thing to be disappointed about. They have no space in their lives for amazement!

I see it all the time during my show. I invite a spectator onstage and ask them to choose a book from a stack on a table. Then have them open the book to any page, look at a word, close the book, and then I read their minds before revealing the word. Pretty good, right? I can't tell you how many people say, "Oh, Jonathan just memorized all the books, and that's how he does it." This is the stunning lack of imagination I'm talking about. Even if that's how I did it (which it's not), that would still be stunning. To memorize the exact contents of thousands of pages of text? That's incredible! But assuming I could do that, it wouldn't give me any indication which of those words my volunteer has chosen. They also assume I have hidden video cameras, hidden assistants, or any number of unimaginative explanations. But, I suppose any answer is good enough for someone lacking curiosity.

I'm not saying they should become my first disciples, but I am saying that any sane person who witnesses something absolutely stunning shouldn't be able to dismiss it so easily. They should spark an intense interest about how something like that could be possible. They should question their own limitations and prejudices about the world. Maybe everything they thought about how the world works was wrong! Given a couple minutes' thought, anyone who witnesses a mental feat like that would enjoy a wonderful exercise in creativity, imagination, and curiosity. You were curious enough to buy this book, so you're on the right track!

Open Your Mind

Don't take anything for granted. Don't assume you

know everything already. Stop occasionally to really ask yourself if you're on the right track. It could be just a minute, but it's time well spent.

Kids are full of wonder. They're interested in everything. They learn at an incredible rate, and I've rarely met a kid who was bored who was free to exercise their curiosity. They're such fast learners because they're curious about everything.

As they grow older, however, we assume we know more and more about how the world works. We get more cynical the more often our expectations are disappointed, and we wind up getting closed off to that all important ingredient: curiosity. If you've lost it, I'm here to tell you nobody else is going to find it for you. It's all up to you!

If you're already curious, and interested in how things work, you've probably been nodding your head in agreement, and will continue to be an interesting person to meet at cocktail parties because you have so much enthusiasm for life.

But, if you're not curious, you're probably thinking, 'That's all well and good for you to say Mr. Mind Reader who has had such an interesting life. But, I'm just not curious about anything, nor have I ever been. That's just the way I am, and that's never going to change. End of story." If that's you, stop it! Remember, whatever you tell yourself is what you believe. So, try this out instead. Try saying, "I've not been curious much before, but I'm going to practice being one starting right now!" With enough conscious effort, you'll quickly find yourself being curious about a number of things as if by. . . habit!

Being curious about things is a good way to discover new hobbies. New groups of people. New skills you never knew you could acquire. And this process is the best way to discover something you're passionate about! So allow yourself to relax the pressure you're putting on yourself to 1) find your passion, and 2) make it your livelihood. There's nothing saying you absolutely have to make money at something you're interested in. Take it from me, demanding money from your interest is a sure-fire way to kill the love you feel for it when it refuses to do so!

Practice Makes Permanent

Hopefully by now you appreciate the difference between pursuing your passion, following your curiosity, and how being curious will get you more out of life than lamenting your lack of passion. It's ok not to have anything you're passionate about. Simply be curious; that's enough to get you moving in the right direction. Don't demand too much of it; let your interest fall to its level and you'll have more than enough material to keep you engaged into your advanced years.

Chapter 13: Gumption

This is one of my favorite words of all times. It's an older word, but I heard it all the time growing up, and I learned to admire the shrewd resourcefulness that it implies. I feel like too many people lack it. They don't have that voice telling them, "You can figure this out." They're too often looking for someone else to save them. Someone else to solve their problems. Someone else to climb their mountain.

Sorry. That's never going to happen. You don't have a savior. You're it. If you aren't saving yourself, ain't nobody else going to step up.

That's the bad news.

The good news is, you can do it. You may not believe in yourself yet, but I already do. Hell, you've gotten this far in the book already. You're clearly capable of enduring extraordinary hardships!

But the difference between where you are right now, and where you'll be a year from now is a measure of what you learn and apply in that time. Most people, though, tend to stop learning the instant they leave school. They think education is a barrier to living. They manage to "just get by." You are different. You recognize that life is the continual process of learning. You know that curiosity, enthusiasm, concentration, creative problem solving, and imagination are all necessary ingredients for success and learning.

Curiosity is the spark, interest & enthusiasm are the fire, concentration & memory are the coals, and accomplishment is the raging inferno that forge success.

We're all capable of learning based on the simple fact that we are born without infinite knowledge. You don't know it all. You literally can't know it all. It's important to recognize this, and also to accept the fact that there are things you don't know, things you can't know, and things you'll never know. If you think about it, there are things you'd like to know, but you're not actually going to invest the time required to do it. And that's ok.

How to Start

What's the difference between the want to learn, and the will to learn? How many times have you thought, "I wish I could do that?" This is the heart of being "interested in being interested." You can wish all day long, but nothing will get done. The will to get something done is the only thing that matters. Wishing is temporary and fleeting. Willingness lasts forever.

If the will to learn is there, you can learn anything. You're not going to start as an expert, and that's ok. At first, your efforts are going to be woefully inadequate compared to your high standards of excellence. Don't be discouraged. The only way to get your skills where you want them is by repeated practice. This is why I suggest people fail small and often. If you put everything you have on a single gamble, you're going to lose. But, if you fail small and often, each one will give you new insight on what to try next time.

Success looks more like crossing the Grand Canyon one step at a time. It's a long hike, but eventually you can climb your way out of the other side. Putting everything into a single gamble is like trying to jump across; it's not going to end well.

With each small win you'll gain more and more confidence in your abilities. This is the heart of gumption. You'll see more and more evidence to bolster your self confidence. The more it happens in one area, the more you start to believe it can happen in others. This is how your whole life gets better; one step forward at a time.

The secret, though, is to just start. If it's a completely new endeavor; start. If it's something you've been in for years; start again. Make the most of your start by giving yourself a direction to work towards. Wandering may not mean you're lost, but it does mean it's going to take longer to get where you're going. And if you tell me that it's not the journey, it's the destination, try telling that to someone who's broke. It's not fun.

Practice Makes [   ]

Repetition is not the secret to success. Perfect repetition makes perfect. If you repeatedly do something the wrong way, you're not improving; you're merely wearing the bad habit into your psyche where it will be more difficult to overcome than if you were starting from scratch. If your belief/approach/strategy is wrong, doing it more isn't going to magically make it right. You might get some results, but the wrong approach will never make you successful on all fronts.

If you want to get better, and make huge advancements, you must be ruthlessly focused on eliminating errors. Search them out. Never turn a blind eye to your shortcomings. Hunt them down. Find them. Dig them up, and throw them away. Look to someone who is better than you at whatever you're learning. Study their approach. See how they do things. Then do what they're doing. This is the best way to learn anything. Direct mentorship is how I learned how to juggle fire when I was 13 years old. I learned how to hammer nails up my nose when I was 15 the same way; someone taught me 1:1. Same goes for eating fire when I was 18. Same goes for performing in colleges. And so on and so on.

Everyone starts as a beginner; even that expert you've put on a pedestal. Sure, there might be a million reasons why you won't make it, but all you need is one reason why you will. Focus on that, and let it move you.

Before You Quit

Learning is hard. Making change is hard. Doing things differently is hard. It's discouraging, for sure. But, if you invite it to live in your mind, you will lose all the progress you've made. Progress is not permanent. It only lasts as long as you continue to cultivate it.

I've learned to identify discouragement as the signal that success is around the corner. Instead of using it as an excuse to quit, I use it to push farther in that direction and things turn out.

I was in the wings waiting to go on stage for America's Got Talent. I had spent the whole day before in front of cameras, following production assistants everywhere, being told where to stand, where to look, who to talk to, and I was tired. It was such a huge emotional strain to be in front of the cameras for that long. All that was weighing on me as I stood waiting for Nick Cannon to tell me, "Ok. Time to go." I wanted to just walk away. I was terrified. Millions of people would be watching me. Waiting for me to fail. Howard Stern, Heidi Klum, Mel B, and Howie Mandel would be looking for any excuse to press their button.

All that was racing through my mind. What would you do in that situation? Any sane person would pull the plug.

Instead, I focused on my breathing and told myself, "This is what I do, now do it." That's gumption. That's confidence.

It only comes through years and years of consistent effort towards a single goal; be the best at what I do. And it worked. I heard my name, Nick gave me thumbs up, and I walked out center stage. The lights were in my eyes, I could see the red dots of cameras everywhere in the darkness, and it was fantastic. For the next 8 minutes I used every single tip, trick, and experience I'd ever had. At the end I got three out of four yesses (Thanks for nothing Howie!), and I was on to the next round!

And that was it. I never got a call back. Turns out, the judges will allow more people through than make it onto the air. This gives the producers more material than they need to create the most compelling narrative for each season's story. What a letdown! All that time, effort, excitement, and emotion to not make it to broadcast.

Talk about discouraging.

But, the experience was invaluable. It was an incredible learning experience, and I use it anytime I talk with TV producers now. It helps me relax. It helps me stay confident. I know what I'm doing. I know I'm good at it. I know it's valuable. No one experience is the be all, end all do-or-die career maker or ender. It's the consistent, daily effort you put in that matters.

Knowledge is Not Power

Now you know the secret to gumption, and it's not knowledge. Enthusiasm without knowledge is like running in the dark, so knowledge is important, but it's mainly potential. Knowledge put into action is the key to success. Take action whenever possible. Don't sit on the sidelines thinking about doing. Too many people are spectators to their life. They allows others to be the main players. They lack gumption.

The best way to learn is by doing. I often tell people they don't truly know something until they can do it. Think about performing a simple magic trick. You might know the "trick" that makes it work, but you can't perform it. Do you really know it, then? Absolutely not! So it goes with what you know only in your head. Until you know it in your bones, and can do it in your sleep, you don't really know something.

Put all that potential to use. Take action. Feed yourself new ideas, and try them out. Give them the road test.

Get serious about your success. It's literally a matter of life and death. Treat your life casually, and you'll soon find it's a casualty. Be systematic about your effort. Constantly strive to improve. The instant you coast is the instant you start losing ground.

Next time you find yourself wishing something, turn that wish into a will to learn, and you're already ahead of 99% of others. Do away with being interested in being interested. Take an active part in your life. Have gumption.

Chapter 14: The All-Seeing Eye of Agamotto

octor Strange is one of my favorite Marvel characters. Formerly a gifted surgeon, and now our world's most talented sorcerer after an unfortunate car accident that puts him on the path to find healing. Along his adventures he comes across a magical amulet called the "Eye of Agamotto," and it has the mystical ability to see across vast distances and dispel disguises and illusions. It sees things as they are; a powerful ability indeed!

After seeing this in the comics as a kid, I imagined how wonderful it would be to have this power, myself. While I may not be able to see into other dimensions, you could say I see more than the average person for sure. Here's how you can, too.

No Sh*t, Sherlock

You may not be as familiar with Doctor Strange, but you've probably heard of Sherlock Holmes; the genius detective. Most people like to think Mentalism is the deductive reasoning of Sherlock Holmes taken to the Nth degree, and they're not too far off the track. You don't have to train your mind to that extent, but I'd wager you could use a tune up.

You know your mind needs to use shortcuts to prevent being overwhelmed, but that means we see millions and millions of details, but we rarely observe those details. You think your senses are there to notice things, but their primary function is to filter out useless information. Too bad it's so good at its job. This is the reason your memory sucks so badly; you probably haven't even been aware of whatever it is you'd like to remember later. The mind must see something first, before your eyes will remember it.

Now, this doesn't mean that you literally can't see something you're unfamiliar with. There's a crazy notion that Native Americans didn't see Columbus's ships because they were completely unfamiliar. This is patently absurd. If this were the literal case, then you'd never see anything because it was all unfamiliar to you at one point.

But, on a smaller scale, in relationships, in business, etc. the mind does have a difficult time seeing something if it doesn't know it exists. For example, there could be evidence galore of treachery, but if you don't know what that evidence looks like, you won't know to see it. In the magic world there are plenty of magic gimmicks that stare you right in the face, but you don't notice them because your mind doesn't know how to interpret what it's seeing as a meaningful detail. Your eyes see it, but your mind doesn't tag it as "important" so it does it's job of filtering out those useless details. Consequently, you're never consciously aware of it, and you can't remember what you never notice. The secret remains a secret while hidden in plain sight.

Practical Demonstrations

If you're still having a hard time wrapping your head around the idea that your senses actively filter out information instead of just gathering as much data for you as possible, let's look at some practical examples. Look at this:

What does it say? "A bird in the hand?" Read it again. I love this test because it's so simple, yet surprising. You mind filters out the "extra" detail, and you don't notice because you're only aware of what your mind allows through the filter. Your sense of sight isn't as passive as you thought!

I've shown this to people who can read it ten times and swear up and down it says "A bird in the hand." But, when I ask them to put their finger on each word as they read it, the extra detail jumps out at them which comes as quite the surprise! You might think this is a cheap trick, and in some ways it is; our minds tend to skip details it thinks it already knows. And that's what I'm trying to show you! It proves that most of us fail to observe what's really going on around us. Ask your friends to read that to you, and you'll have to agree.

This plays out in thousands of ways every day. I saw it consistently when I worked at Disney World. For a short time I was a safari driver at Kilimanjaro Safaris, the most popular attraction at Animal Kingdom, and it was a fantastic experience! One of my favorite off-duty pranks was to go to the parks with five or six friends. We'd start a line, and faster than you'd believe possible, complete strangers would start lining up behind us. We could then leave the queue and ask people farther back, "Hey, what are you in line for?" They wouldn't know, but they sure were excited for it! We'd let them off the hook and we'd all have a good laugh about it.

I also see this while riding public transit here in Chicago. A train will let out, and hundreds of people clog up at the station's exit trying to get through a single door with several others just a few feet away completely unused! Nobody sees them. They notice what everyone else is doing, and decide that's good enough for them. They fail to observe the unused exits because they're so plainly obvious, familiar, and nondescript.

If you're back to thinking that would never happen to you, let me ask you this. Do you know what color underwear you're wearing right now? Do you know if you turn your house key clockwise, or counterclockwise to lock it? Do you know if the number 4 on your watch is an Arabic number four, or is it a Roman numeral? (If it's a Roman numeral that's probably a double trick question. Often it won't be "IV," the proper way to write 4 in numerals. Instead it will sometimes be "IIII.")

The list of questions could go on forever. Point being, we could use some help in the observation department. The best place to start is learning how to be attentive, be present, and be aware of where you are. This is phenomenally difficult. Too often we're in our heads, caught up in our thoughts instead of living in the moment. This is why the chapter on concentration is so important.

Here's an exercise. Get a pen and a piece of paper, and think about one of the rooms where you live. Try to list everything in it that you can remember. Then walk in there and check your list. Notice as much as you can. Go back to your list and try again. You'll likely include more items now. The list will get longer and longer as you check your work repeatedly. Try it with a different room. You'll find your first list gets longer and longer as you develop the habit of really noticing what you're looking at.

Another way to practice is to draw what you see. It's not easy! The reason it's so difficult is that the connection between your eyes and your hand has to pass through your brain, and your brain prefers to deal with symbols instead of reality. Things are easier that way. So you'll see the delicate curves and lines of your house plant, and your brain says, "Ah! I know what 'houseplant' looks like!" and it tells your hand to draw the symbol for "houseplant."

No wonder your drawings look like a child did it; your brain started cataloguing symbols when you were a child! That's why drawing from life is such a good practice in observation. In order to draw what's really there, you must ignore the tendency your mind has to assume it knows what to see. The better your powers of observation, the better your drawings will get. It's not your hand that is the problem; it's your mind.

Chapter 15: Superhuman Memory

I'm going to show you how to remember anything. Not everything, mind you, but anything you genuinely want to remember. This will function as a primer on how our memory works, how to improve it, and how it can go wrong; but if you're interested in learning more, you can check one of my other books, Perfect Recall, for a more in-depth exploration of memory.

But it all boils down to this: in order to remember something, you must first be aware of it. That's why we just went over the importance of observation in the previous chapter; you can't remember what you never observed!

Memory Is Fallible

Most people tend to think of their memory as a high quality video replay of what they've experienced. Turns out, this couldn't be farther from the truth. Elizabeth Loftus is a psychology researcher specializing in understanding the nature of memory. Her expertise? Helping people remember something that never happened. She's done a lot of work showing how easy it is to plant false memories, and how eyewitness testimony is next to worthless even when the witness knows for sure what happened. Certainty has almost zero correlation to the accuracy of memory. You can feel like you remember it 100 percent right, and be almost 100 percent wrong.

And magicians have known this for thousands of years. One of my favorite things is talking with people after one of my shows, and listening to them explain what they just saw. Their memory of the event is always wildly inaccurate. They remember effects I never did, they don't remember me doing things that would explain a mystery; and the more time that passes, the greater this effect will become. Eventually they're going to remember that one time I conjured a demon, and I'm 100 percent certain I've never done that.

How does this happen? It's a natural tendency that I help out with conscious effort. In the course of performing a routine we will have all the fun by-play that makes the whole thing work, and then I "helpfully" recap what we've all just seen happen. In this retelling of the experience, I will neglect to mention certain things, or suggest that some things happened that never actually happened; and this is what's remembered by the audience. Our brains are always looking for the easy way out; and when the whole package is put together with a tidy bow by me, the performer, the audiences' brains will prefer that narrative to the exclusion of their own experience.

This happens to even the most skeptical viewer!

You can use this to your own advantage when you do the mind reading trick using this book! You have to turn your head back to glimpse the word, but you're doing it under the guise of asking them if they have the word in mind before you turn your head away again. Once the book is closed and put away you can say, "Here's where we are. I flipped through the book, you said stop, you looked at a word, and I closed the book. My head was turned away the whole time, and you're the only person in the world who could know what the word is, right?" Now, when the person tries to remember what happened, they're going to remember the edited version that conforms to what you told them. This is the heart of the misinformation effect that has been studied extensively by Elizabeth Loftus.

The next time you're in an argument with your sweetie about something you know for sure you remember correctly, it's probably best to admit you might be wrong. You'll be a lot happier then.

Improved Recall

Now that you're more aware of how crappy your memory actually is, we can move on to improving your recall. This is not an exact science! You will, however, have a more accurate memory of the details you want to remember, as they actually happened compared to most people.

Applying any system works better when you understand the principles it operates on. You know your memory system is vulnerable to after-the-fact editing and influence based on the words used to describe an event. Your memory of an event is also influenced by the emotional state you're in at the time of recall. Your current feelings will "rub off" on whatever it is you're remembering. Sleep deprivation also will impair your ability to accurately recall information. I know I'm going to have a rough show anytime I haven't gotten a lot of sleep. When a significant percentage of my success relies on being able to remember multiple pieces of information I see for three seconds, that's a big drawback. So get your sleep.

The things we remember most easily are usually related to ideas, concepts, or details that you're already familiar with. This why a new detail on a topic you know already is much easier to recall than a detail on a topic you have no experience with. What you need to do is develop a system that allows you to associate any kind of new information in an easy-to-recall way. This is called Mnemonics.

Mnemonics is the application of fundamental memory principles to improve your recall. When used properly, any mnemonic system will leverage evolutionary biases in your favor. That means creating vivid mental imagery in a way your brain can't help but remember forever. The more vivid the better. The more outrageous, the better. The more ridiculous, the better. The more violent, the better. The more your mental picture plays with scale (either too big or too small), the better. The more illogical, the better. These are all things that, in the real world, your brain would attach significant importance to! Now, instead of subconsciously creating mental associations between details, we're going to make your brain do it with intention.

Practice

Remember this list of ten items: Mug, towel, thumbdrive, knife, playing card, bottle, tree, earbuds, shoebox, magnet.

With no training, how long do you think it would take you to remember this list? Can you do it now without looking back at them a second time? Probably not. But I'm going to show you a simple method that will help you recall them in order, forward, backwards, or in any sequence you like using a rhyming mnemonic system. Here's how it works.

Once you learn the structure I'm about to tell you, never change it. It will stay the same forever and always. This will be the rock solid base that you "link" new information to using ridiculous associations.

Here it is:

1. Gun
2. Shoe
3. Tree
4. Door
5. Hive
6. Tricks
7. Heaven
8. Gate
9. Wine
10. Hen

Notice these items rhyme with the number they're associated with. One/Gun. Two/Shoe. Three/Tree. And so on. This turns each number into an easy-to-remember picture. Now, for the first item on the list you're trying to remember, mug. Link it in your mind to Gun. The weirder the association, the better. Really see the picture in your mind. If you skip this step, you won't remember it later. It has to be distinct and unusual to work. Once you have it, let it go. It will be back when you need it, but for now you can be sure mug is linked to gun.

Do this process with the other items. Link each item in the list to the corresponding item for its number. I'm purposefully avoiding giving you any example associations because whatever you choose to think up will be easier for you to recall when you need it. The important thing is actually using your imagination to create as vivid an image in your mind as you can before moving on. With just a little practice you can create these associations almost as fast as people can toss out suggestions. But for now, stick to the list of ten items I've already given you.

Once you have each item associated to a number, all someone has to do is ask you, "What's at number one?" and you think, "One > Gun > Mug!" You know mug is the right answer. Someone says "How about number nine?" You think, "Nine > Wine > Shoe box!" Your mind's tendency to remember things that rhyme combined with your bizarre mental pictures is all you need to recall the list forwards, backwards, or in any order. This is a technique that works no matter how tired you are, too! I used to do this all the time in college at parties. No matter how much punch I'd drank, I could still recall things people called out. I'd just have to make sure they wrote it down so they would remember! Now you know my secret. Use it wisely, and amaze all your friends.

Now, hopefully, you see how simple improving your recall can be if you apply a little imagination combined with organization. Before now, I bet you thought you were going to live the rest of your life with a horrible memory! But now you have a simple yet effective technique for remembering a list of items, chores, shopping lists, and so on. If this kind of thing is something that seriously interests you, and you want to continue your studies, I strongly suggest you check out my book Perfect Recall, which goes more in depth on the history of memory systems, linking, peg systems, and the like, available at Amazon.

Chapter 16: Be Likeable

Too many people believe it's their talents that will lead to success, when there's actually one thing that matters above all else: being likeable! I shared this Carl W. Buehner quote already in Chapter 11, but it's too good not to share again here: "They may forget what you said — but they will never forget how you made them feel."

In your day-to-day life, nobody really cares whether you're in the top 99 percentile of your age bracket for underwater basket weaving. They don't care. That talent doesn't matter. What does matter is being able to connect with strangers as quickly as possible in a genuine, friendly, positive way. We call this being likeable. Nail that and everything else falls into place. I can't tell you how many upgrades, freebies, opportunities, and perks I've enjoyed over the years by virtue of being the only positive interaction someone has had during their workday. It pays to be liked!

In general, people want to like other people. And make no mistake, we're talking about real life connections here, not just Facebook likes! We're going to talk about how to connect with people in meatspace, which still has a lot of value; maybe even more now that most prefer to stay in the virtual world!

Jonathan **Pritchard**

What you say, what you do, and what you wear are the three biggest things that impact how others evaluate whether or not they should like you. What controls those three things? How you think about them, of course! It's not an easy job to give you a personality overhaul in a single chapter, but I'm not one to back down from a challenge!

Learn How to Like Others

You're never going to get something without giving something. That's true in this arena, too. If you want others to like you, you have to like them first. The best way to do that is to be more interested than interesting. Be interested in what they're interested in. Ask questions about their interests. This is the absolute fastest way to get someone's attention in a positive way. Everyone wants to feel appreciated. Everyone wants to be wanted. When you ask someone about something they're interested in, you make them feel seen. Who wouldn't love someone who makes them feel like that?! Anyone who says they don't need it, I think.

I can't tell you how many friends I've made (and kept for years!) after a single interaction where I simply got interested in what they have going on in their life. I ask about their problems. Their wins. Their friends. Their family. Their memories. Anything and everything is fair game! Just remember, this is not actually a game.

These are real people you're talking to. I like the way Bob Marley put it: "The biggest coward is a man who awakens a woman's love with no intentions of loving her." The sentiment applies here. You're not connecting with people to get something from them. Instead, you're focused on what you can give them, even if it's as simple as a moment of your attention. And that is precious indeed!

You have to learn how to genuinely like people in order to really, truly connect with them. Artifice will only get you so far. People can sense fakeness from a mile away. Try to cheat your way in, and you're going to lose every time. Just remember that people will treat you just like you treat them. That's why I like to say that the only person you meet is yourself. You can prove it to yourself, too! Instead of smiling at the next person you meet, scowl at them. See what happens! They're likely to return the favor! People respond to what you're broadcasting at all times. They're like mirrors for your inner emotions. When you really wrap your head around this, you'll realize you can either be responsible for spreading your frustrations, anger and hatred, which makes the world a worse place to live; or you can choose to focus on transmitting happiness, positivity, and hope. That's what I want!

The people who are the most cynical of that idea are usually the ones who are the most lonely. They've made a habit out of isolating themselves as protection.

Instead of reaching out to people who could help, they choose to build walls. If that's you, remember that you have a choice. Since you're the person who built the walls, you can bring them down, too. You can choose to build bridges instead. The fastest way to do that? Show the world some warmth.

Be A Friend

Be the friend you wish you had. Make it your mission to show the kind of love and support you want in your own life. You have to be an example of how you want others to treat you. You can't demand more from others than you're willing to give yourself! I have the best friends in the world, and they've given me more than I could ever repay them, but that sure as hell doesn't mean I'm not going to try. Share your light with the world, and there's more light; doesn't diminish your fire any!

Whatever excuse you have for not being a friend to the world is just that, an excuse. There's always time for kindness. I don't care if you're sick, worried, or what; nobody deserves to have your problems dumped in their lap. That's your shit. Own it. Maybe you feel like the whole world is out to get you. Here's what I say to that. If you meet an asshole in the morning, you met an asshole. If you meet nothing but assholes all day, you're the asshole. If you don't like yourself, there's no amount of smiling at others that's going to fix it. You gotta work on all that baggage you've been carrying around everywhere you go.

Laugh At Yourself

If you take all this stuff SO SERIOUSLY, you're going to miss out on a lot of the fun of being alive! Have a sense of humor about life. You're not getting out of here alive; better to go through it laughing! If you can't laugh at yourself, you can be sure others will do the honors for you.

People love being around someone who can make them laugh. It helps them feel less nervous. Less anxious. More at ease. If you have a sense of humor, you'll be wanted everywhere you go. Just like everything we've talked about already, it's a skill of the mind — that's it! Focus on what you can do to the world more than what the world is doing to you, and you'll find plenty to laugh at! A sense of humor will help you cope with problems you'd otherwise allow to grow into monsters by constantly ignoring them. Admit them with a smile, and you rob them of their power to get stronger.

Know Your Humors

Not all sarcasm is created equal! Most people who use sarcasm are using it as a defense mechanism. They're wielding their intellect as a weapon, cutting others down in an attempt to make themselves feel bigger.

This is the wrong approach. Build others up. Use your smarts to find ways to encourage others. You never lose anything by encouraging others to succeed. Sarcasm is rarely the best tool for the job.

I get it, though. You think it's blatantly obvious that you'd never consider your friends idiots; but if the only thing you ever call your friends is idiots, what do they have to go on? So be sure that your tongue-in-cheek way of playfully putting others down isn't mistaken for the genuine article. Use humor to build people up, never cut them down. As a general rule, I cut sarcasm completely out of my tool kit. The drawbacks vastly outweigh the benefits. I prefer an honest, positive approach!

Talk the Talk

How much talking do you do? This is the main way most people judge your personality. Do you blather on for hours without taking a breath? Do you go into every single detail about a topic regardless of how desperately your victim is trying to escape the "conversation?"

I've found value in noting that we have two ears and one mouth, and therefore can do twice the amount of listening as talking. I also go by this rule as much as possible; if you can't say anything nice, say nothing. It's so much easier to tear down than it is to build up, and

I refuse to contribute. People notice if you're overly critical, and they can't help but think, "I wonder what he's going to say about me when I leave?"

Also, how much do you talk about yourself? As surprising as it may seem, I try to avoid it as much as possible! I've heard my stories before. I'd rather hear a story I don't know inside and out already. The only way I can make sure that happens is to ask someone about their favorite subject: them!

Are you too nervous to talk to people? Do you stare at the floor when you do muster up the courage to have a conversation? The best place to look when you're talking to someone is right at 'em. Look them right in the eyes! If this makes you uncomfortable, like it did me when I was growing up, you can do what I did: get used to looking at yourself in the mirror. Look right into your own eyes. You know the person looking back. Be nice to each other. Before long, you'll find it's not so bad.

Realize, though, there's a fine line. Lock eyes too long, it can come across as a challenge or threat. Especially to gorillas. Never look a gorilla in the eyes. This is a problem rarely encountered at brunch, so you don't need to devote a lot of brainpower to remembering it. You'll just be happier to have that piece of trivia and not need it than you would to need it and not have it.

Listen With Your Whole Mind

Listening to someone tells them that what they have to say is important to you. Don't just listen with your ears. Listen with your whole body. Listen to understand them better. Nod when you understand something. Show confusion if you need more explanation. Smile when they say something funny. Don't be passive. Don't just listen for your turn to jump in.

If you stop listening, you're bored. And here's a revelation: it's never that you're bored with them, or what they're talking about. You're bored with yourself. You're frustrated at allowing yourself to be in that situation. Don't put that on them; they didn't ask for it!

Don't Be So Honest

"I'm just being honest" is the distinctive call of the insensitive prick; a particularly small creature who constantly feels the need to use honesty as a disguise for their terrifying lack of self-confidence.

Strangers aren't always honest with you. Your friends aren't always honest with you. Your family isn't always honest with you. Your sweetie isn't always honest with you. You aren't always honest with yourself! And that's okay. Honesty is expensive. You've paid for this book, so I'm giving you my honest opinion. Otherwise I'd just be smiling and nodding at you right now. And that's the truth!

Your Battlecry

When you see someone you know, do you shout, "There you are!" Or, "Here I am!" Which do you think they would be more happy to hear?

Everything we've been talking about are essentially ways of making other people's interests your interests. Everybody has just as strong a desire to be loved, accepted, and welcomed as you have, so the best place to start is showing the type of consideration you'd like to see for yourself. Be the change you want to see in the world, in others, and in yourself!

Know A Little Something About Everything

A little bit of geography can help you connect with someone about how wonderful their hometown is. Maybe you had a childhood friend who liked to build model rockets just like the person you just met. Maybe you have a current friend who once worked at Disney World, and you can share a detail they told you with the family you see getting ready for their flight to Orlando.

How broad are your interests? I believe it's supremely

important to know a little bit about everything, so that you have more potential ways to find common ground with someone. This is distinctly different from being a know-it-all! You are not auditioning for Jeopardy. You are simply looking for some kind of connection with this human being you're talking to.

If you spend your time learning about the same three topics, you're going to be desperately underprepared to meet new people. This is a big problem in the magic world. Too many magicians never take a moment to poke their head into any other performing art! They could find so much inspiration if they simply went to the opera once a year! Instead, they can only talk about their interests, and they wonder why the 15th card trick hasn't gotten them a friend yet. Some of my best magician friends haven't shown me a magic trick in ten years, and we love it that way; we like to talk about other stuff!

But you can't talk about other stuff if you never learn about other stuff. Broaden your horizons. Expand your mind. Learn something completely new!

The Secret

Everything in this chapter could basically be said as, "Like yourself, and get along with others." Simple to say, often the most difficult thing to do!

Chapter 17: Public Speaking

I used to be so shy I wouldn't even ask for ketchup at Wendy's. Ask my mom; she loves to tell people the story. I hated talking to strangers, and it made me feel uncomfortable. Then I started seeing how it was the outgoing people who seemed to make friends easily and be popular, and I knew I'd have to come out of my shell if I wanted to make more friends, too.

I started juggling when I was thirteen, and this allowed me to demonstrate skill in front of a crowd of people without having to say anything. I wouldn't have to engage with anyone; I could still stay in my bubble but people would give me positive feedback in the form of applause. With direction from my first mentor I included "patter" (the industry term for a script). It consisted of age-old jokes, gags, and bits of business. It was easy because I didn't have to come up with anything original; I just said what my mentor told me to say, and things worked!

About this same time I realized I think almost entirely in pictures. I see ideas as images, movies, and scenes in my brain. This is a benefit that helped me when I went to college for art, but back in junior high I'd be in the middle of a conversation, have a really good idea, and then take three days to translate the image I saw in my mind to words, and then remind the person about the conversation we had three days ago and explain the idea. Not the best way to communicate!

I'd already seen the value in being able to stand up in front of a group of people with juggling; and being able to say a couple things that made them laugh was even better. That's why I decided to devote every elective I had in high school to taking Speech & Debate. Almost every weekend for the next three years was devoted to attending and competing in debate tournaments. I became a member of the National Forensics League (I'm in the NFL!), and my preferred event was Lincoln-Douglas Debate. These are always topics dealing with moral obligation and "should" moreseo than issues of policy or "how." There would be a resolution like "Resolved: A just government ought to prioritize civil liberties over national security," and then you'd have to build an argument for the resolution (Affirmative) and build an argument against the resolution (Negative). At the debate, you never know which side you'll be on, so you have to be prepared for both!

If you're Affirmative you go first, and you get a couple minutes to present your reasoning why we should support the resolution. Then the Negative debater gets a couple minutes to ask you clarifying questions to make sure they understand your position. Then they have the opportunity to make their case. They can choose to focus solely on refuting your arguments, or simply presenting their own arguments against the resolution. The rest of the exchange is focused on showing why the other person is wrong, and why you're right, in the most compelling, persuasive manner as you can.

I loved it! It forced me to quickly be able to translate the images in my mind into words that I could use to persuade someone to my point of view. Then I could switch sides, and do it all over again! This is the foundation that my whole career is built on.

After high school I continued performing for larger and larger audiences, and when I graduated I went on tour with a full-time magician who was active in the college market. I would open for him, and this gave me time in front of even bigger audiences to hone my skills. Then for the next ten years I was out performing by myself for audiences of all sizes, and getting more and more comfortable on stage. That's how I could walk out on stage for the TV show America's Got Talent and have a blast during the whole thing.

Your Situation

You probably don't have twenty years' worth of public speaking and presenting skills under your belt, and that's okay! The good news is that you can learn this stuff pretty easily. The main secret is that, everyone else is so terrified of it, even the lowest bar is still amazing to most.

How many times have you had to share something with your team? That's public speaking. Have you ever delivered sales numbers to your boss? That's public speaking. Ever had to pitch your company's services to a prospective client? That's public speaking!

People who can speak with confidence get more out of their job. Every speaking opportunity is a leadership opportunity, a business opportunity, and a career opportunity.

"Aren't You Nervous?!"

This is the number one reason don't like speaking in front of others; they're afraid, for which I have two responses. First, if you weren't qualified to talk about whatever you're being asked to talk about, you probably wouldn't have been asked to talk about it. You know your stuff, and that's why you're being asked to be there. Competence is a big part of confidence. Second, feel the nervousness and do it anyway.

There's a strange thing about being nervous; in physiological terms, the measurements are exactly the same as when you're excited for something you really enjoy. That means your hands sweat, your heart rate skyrockets, your stomach does flip-flops, and your whole body goes tingly, for both good and bad things. The only difference is how you choose to interpret those physical cues.

If you're scared to speak, you'll interpret those physical signs as a bad thing. If you're excited to go on a first date, you'll interpret those physical signs as a good thing. The choice is yours! So, here's a trick I used when my body was going haywire waiting to go out on stage for America's Got Talent. Tell yourself you're excited to do your best. Don't try to stop the sensations; ride the wave!

Look At Others

Another fear people tell me they have is of having so many people look at them. "They're all judging me!" they say. Well, that says more about you and what you're thinking than what the audience is thinking. You aren't a professional mind reader! You don't know what's going through their heads. Anything you imagine they're thinking is actually your own thoughts being projected "out there." It feels like it's coming from somewhere else, but it's really your own energy that you're perceiving as external.

If you're worried everyone is judging you, that means you're not admitting to yourself how much you judge others. If you feel like everyone is staring at you, it's your own desire to check them out which you don't feel comfortable owning. Any psychological pressure you feel from an outside source is actually some form of your own coming back at you that you're not conscious of.

When I was starting out, I always felt like people were staring at me, and I hated it. Once I realized I really was interested in other people, and wanted to check them out, my awkwardness disappeared completely. I reclaimed that part of my personality that I wasn't comfortable with before and made friends with it, and now it's one of my strongest traits!

The Secret of Comedy Is...

...timing. Same goes for speaking. The only thing you should actually be scared of is going on too long when you speak. This is the absolute worst amatuer mistake and I see it all the time with people who do introductions. They get a mic in their hands and out comes the verbal diarrhea! They ramble on and on, getting no closer to the point. Don't be that person! Know what you're going to say, say it, and get on with it! Keep your talk short, to the point, and leave your audience wanting more. It's always better to be asked back a second time than to use up all your goodwill at once.

Going over your time is an egregious error and the mark of a beginner. I've seen plenty of performers on a group show go twenty minutes over their allotted time because "Boy! They were loving me, so I had to keep going!" They've stolen time from the other acts, and they're rarely invited back. In the world of television, that kind of behavior is even worse; because when they say you have three minutes and twenty seconds they mean you have three minutes and twenty seconds. Not 3:17. Not 3:24. 3:20! If you're talking to your coworkers you probably won't be working with such tight schedules, but the lesson stays the same; respect the audience's time and stick to the point. Get up, speak up, shut up.

Plan for Success

The best way to make the most out of your speaking time is to plan accordingly. Know what you're going to say before you say it. Even the most off-the-cuff speeches you can point to were probably meticulously crafted for that effect. It takes practice to appear that unpracticed! The best trick is to know the main points you'd like to cover, prepare a couple points on each, and write it all down in an outline. This is a good balance between extemporaneous speaking and reading off a piece of paper. Both are equally as bad! Instead, you'll have a loose structure to keep you on track, and it will prevent you from droning on like most people do when reading a prepared statement word for word.

This is how I would build my debate cases. I'd have a single word to represent the whole thought I wanted to talk about. Once I got to the end of that thought, I'd look at my notes to see what the next word was, and that would trigger the whole next thought. Using this method can condense quite a bit of information into a single notecard.

Point of information: Use cardstock for your notes. If you're holding a piece of paper and your hands are shaking, the flimsy paper will amplify the effect, making it much more noticeable. You'll appear nervous, the audience will notice, and you'll notice the audience noticing, and so begins the negative feedback loop of the flop-sweats. Card stock doesn't do this, so even if your hands are shaking a little bit, it will be much less noticeable!

Be The Captain

No matter what stage you're on, you're in charge of the experience for the audience. Your job is to manage that dynamic with grace, confidence, and assurance. This will help put the audience at ease, and they will be able to focus on what you have to say. Stand in one place, and don't pace. Speak clearly and loudly. Use a microphone at all times if available. Look everyone in the eye as you scan the room. Remember to smile!

Imagine you're the pilot of an airplane that's about to take off. You hop on the intercom and say, "Uhhhh, hi, uuhhhhhhh everyone. Uhhh, I think, well, yeah! Yeah, we're going to uhmmmmm, Phoenix? Today? Yeah. Phoenix. Okay, all right, yeah. So, just sit back, and relax while, uhmmmm, what? Right! Yeah, relax while I figure this thing out!" They wouldn't be able to get off that plane fast enough! That does not instill confidence in your passengers!

So, when you stand on stage, own the job! Accept the responsibility, and respect your audience enough to prepare for the experience. Lack of preparation shows a complete disdain for the people who are looking to you for guidance. If you have to make a presentation, but you're still unsure about how well you'll do, don't wait; just do it! If you never try you'll never fail, but you'll also never succeed. Don't worry about it too much; just get out there and do it. The second time will be better than your first. And your third time will be worse than your second because you'll get cocky. You'll figure that out, and your fourth time will be the best one yet!

Chapter 18: Worry

Imagine there's a huge balloon with a hole in it. Eventually that balloon will lose all its air, and be completely deflated. That's what worry does to your energy. Worry robs you of the ability to take action. It quietly bleeds your gumption away until you're left with nothing but crippling stress. Worry is essentially the mental capacity to not take action. Worry is the experience of fear over an event which hasn't happened yet.

That's pretty amazing, too. I'm a professional mind reader, and I'm really bad at forecasting the future. Sure, I can make reasonable guesses about what's going to happen this afternoon, but tomorrow? Forget about it! Who knows what's going to happen? I sure don't. I'll be too busy making choices, taking action, and getting shit done to worry about what could happen.

Now, I know telling you not to worry is about as effective as telling you not to breathe. Never going to happen. But, I can show you why most worrying is a waste of your mental energy. Not only is worrying less than effective, it can actively do you harm.

Worry is a poor use of your imagination. You're devoting your mental creativity to conjuring imaginary worst-case scenarios instead of putting that same energy into encouraging yourself, or finding creative solutions to the problems you're facing.

Origins of Worry

Worrying makes evolutionary sense. It's a good motivator to find solutions now for problems in the future. You could say squirrels worry about the coming winter so they store acorns now. Bears worry about the coming winter and they get fat by eating lots of salmon now. There are clouds in the distance, and you worry about what all that rain is going to do when it gets here, so you build a shelter now.

So, worry makes sense. It really does. It helps you find solutions now for future problems while you still have time to do something about it. The problem happens when worry robs you of the ability to take action. Plus, nowadays we live in a world where we have same-day delivery from Amazon. Almost any problem you can imagine has a simple solution. And that's assuming the problem is actually going to happen!

Exercise

You won't believe it until you see it, so prove it to yourself. Get a piece of paper and write down every single thing you're worried about. Every one. Don't skip any. Don't do this on a computer, really use paper. It has to be physical! You have to see your worries in your handwriting. You have to own them. Now, put it somewhere safe for a couple months. Set a reminder on your phone, "Check my page of worries that I hid between pages 24 & 25 in the third book on the second shelf." I bet you dollars to donuts that most of the things that you were worried about never happened. Or, if they did actually happen, they weren't nearly as bad as your imagination made them out to be.

Dread is always worse than the experience. Anyone can endure pain. You have to. But dread can kill you. That's why worry is lethal to your creativity, happiness, and willingness to connect with others.

It takes a lot of gumption to admit that pain is unavoidable in life. So is frustration. And disappointment. And sadness. But that's the way of the world. You can endure it because you have to. Don't allow your mind to become your tormentor. Make a friend out of it. Tell your worrying mind that you appreciate its concern for your well-being, and that you recognize it's trying to help you avoid pain in the future. Accept that this is the best way it knows how to care for you, and that it all comes from a place of love. Don't try to fight it; dissolve the struggle completely by embracing it. You don't have time to fight yourself. If there's something to be done about a problem, take action. Do something about it. You can't afford to use your mental power to fight itself. Self-destruction rarely builds success.

Jonathan **Pritchard**

Endure the Worst

I once got booed by 1,200 people. The complete story is a 45-minute comedy of errors, but the main takeaway is that I screwed up every single thing that could have possibly gone wrong, for an opportunity that could have gotten me more work than I could handle for the next couple years. Instead, I crashed and burned completely.

My performer friends all like to swap horror stories from the road when we hang out together. Everyone agrees this is one of the worst they've ever heard. And you know what? It wasn't that bad. I got through it. It was awful in the moment, but now it makes for a great story. Sure, I missed some major opportunities, but the fall-out wasn't nearly as bad as I feared.

I used to wonder what would happen if I completely failed a performance. Now I know! And it's not that bad. I've been through the worst I could ever have imagined, and now I'm bulletproof. Long story short; nobody was bleeding, and I'm the only person who wound up crying. It wasn't that bad.

Imagine the worst-case scenario, take appropriate action to prepare for it, and then move on. Let the worry spur action, and nothing more. Remember that failure is always an option — in fact, it's sometimes the easiest option — but the only time you fail is when you don't learn the lesson from the experience. That's why all my failures are called "opportunities for learning." I don't worry about failing anymore; I look forward to learning!

Death From A Thousand Cuts

Most of your worries aren't life or death situations. They aren't. In the grand scheme of things, most of your worries are small potatoes. You're worried about being late to something. You're worried someone isn't going to like you. You're worried the store is going to be out of your favorite ice cream.

So where's the value? Where's the reward in this worrying behavior? Well, it makes you feel like you're significant. It makes you feel like your life matters because this ice cream flavor is a very important matter. But this is not a positive use of your creativity. You're killing your motivation, gumption, and confidence by a thousand worrisome cuts.

Prepare for the unexpected, then move on. You may not be able to prevent inconveniences, but you can stop them from setting up shop in your imagination where they will feed like a tick on your mental energies. If the situation is a big deal, then there's either something you can do about it, or there isn't. Do what you can, and forget about the rest!

Jonathan **Pritchard**

Stop Feeding the Monster

How often do you complain about your worries? Are you constantly complaining to your friends, your spouse, or your family? Stop it. This does absolutely nothing to alleviate your worries. Only action can fix it. When you complain to others, the only thing you're doing is spreading negativity, perpetuating your focus on the problem, and subtly influencing others to fixate on their problems, too. They aren't professional therapists; stop talking to them like one! If they are, at least pay them for the privilege of dumping your emotional garbage on them!

Chapter 19: The Mind-Killer

This passage from Frank Herbert's Dune has me throwing praise hands in the air.

"I must not fear. Fear is the mind-killer. Fear is the little-death that brings total obliteration. I will face my fear. I will permit it to pass over me and through me. And when it has gone past I will turn the inner eye to see its path. Where the fear has gone there will be nothing. Only I will remain."

Damn! Who knew sci-fi could preach like that?!

In some cases fear is a good thing. Strange noise in the grass? Might be a tiger, so let's let that fear trigger a whole bunch of adrenaline so we can run away as fast as we can. This is an example of rational fear. Useful fear.

Anyone who says they're 100 percent fearless is either stupid, unimaginative, or has simply given up the will to live. Fear, like pain, is sometimes a good signal that something needs your attention, and now! Fear teaches you to respect dangers like ignorance, illness, reckless behaviors, etc. Fear, in these instances, has done more good than harm over history. It's helped create educational systems, vaccines, safety measures, and the like.

The fear we must manage are the irrational ones. We are much more likely to be killed by heart disease than an airplane falling out of the sky, but I can tell you which one I'm more scared of. Most people are terrified of public speaking despite it being one of the best opportunities to be seen as a leader and expert in your field. People are scared of dying! You know what, though? I don't remember where I was before I was born, so I'm probably not going to remember where I am after I'm gone, either. I'm not looking forward to the process of dying, but I don't think I'll mind being dead once I'm there.

Fear As A Tool

Just like with money, fear makes a better servant than master. Learn to make your fear work for you. The bravest people you've ever seen were scared out of their minds. Then they went ahead and did what they did anyway. They simply didn't allow fear to keep them from taking action.

Over the years of your life you're going to face any number of situations and experiences that will scare you. There's nothing to be ashamed of about being scared, but don't let it call the shots. It's like a puppy running through a screen door. At first it may not cause much damage, but if you allow it to continue, there will soon be a giant hole and you'll have to go chasing after it. The puppy will be in the lead. Same for your fears. Train them. Take ownership of them. Don't let them run rampant in your mind.

Do the thing that scares you. It's the unknown that really frightens you. So go ahead and try it once so you know exactly what tricks it has up its sleeves. You might be surprised how much you can enjoy it! I used to be scared to talk to people; now it's one of my favorite things!

Lying to yourself doesn't work, either. Trying to ignore your fears keeps them hidden in the corners of your mind where they can multiply and thrive. Bring them to the forefront instead. Call attention to them. Boldly name them, and gain power over them! If the fear persists, accept its place in your mind, and act anyway! Fear rarely survives action. Remember, stop being a spectator in your own adventure. Take part in your life! Be bold, do something about it! You might just be afraid you'll like it.

Try It For Two Days

Give yourself two days to be free of your fears. Just two days, that's it! Then you can get right back into it. But I'd wager that those two days will be more productive and happy than any you've had for awhile. The two days I suggest keeping free of fear would be today and tomorrow. The day after that you can get back to it!

Chapter 20: Positive Thinking Positively Sucks

I hate most motivational speakers with an unholy passion. They come breezing in, give a rah-rah speech that's supposed to get you fired up about your shitty job, and then accept their $20,000 fee before disappearing into the night. Then two weeks later, the sales numbers are down again because you've realized it was all hogwash.

Positive thinking is useless.

That might be strange to say near the end of a book written by a mind reader, but there you have it. We've covered a lot of ground about mindset, and the power of thought, so what in the world am I talking about?

Not one thought I've shared, not one piece of advice, nor one insight I've had is worth a damn if you don't do something with it. If you read this book, put it back on the shelf, and never take action, you will have wasted your time, and I will have wasted my time in writing it for you.

I've spend hundreds of pages talking about how important it is to get your mind right for the sole purpose of getting you to the point where you realize it's not in the knowing; it's in the doing. Want to improve your life? Do something that will make it better.

You can't hope, wish, or pray your way to a better life. The only thing that matters in your life and this universe is what actually happens. Not what could have happened. Not what might happen. What. Actually. Happens.

And you can choose what that is through the application of your mental powers to direct your efforts. That's how the mind can change the world; by efficient use of your potential.

Actions Speak Louder Than Words

Words are just audible thoughts. They're practically useless; they can't knock over a fly! In the well-adjusted person of society, the longer they focus on their problems and imaginary issues, the more power they steal, and the stronger they become. This is the threat of indecision. More squirrels are killed by indecision than are by running across the road. If they picked a side and went for it, there were be a lot less roadkill. Talking about a problem does nothing to solve it, if it's not focusing on finding and enacting a solution.

Be realistic about your situation; I'm not talking about putting your head in the clouds. But the more you act, the happier you'll be. Don't just respond to you environment. Practice imposing your will on your life. It's your life, own it!

The Obstacle Is The Way

Too many people try to escape their situation instead of capitalizing on it. Appreciate where you are. Consider your problems. Learn from them. Thank them for the lessons they're trying to teach you. Show them respect by actually learning those lessons!

You're never going to be rid of problems completely; you'll just level up to more and more interesting problems. There's nothing worse that I can imagine than having the same problems for more than a year. But they're there to test your resolve. To forge your willpower and willingness to take action.

Winning in life isn't in the outcome, but in putting forth the effort in the first place. I don't care if you're not going to be perfect the first time you try something. I care about you trying in the first place. Say yes, and figure it out later. The biggest wins I've ever had felt like they were too big, and if I had stayed the same person they would have been. Instead I say yes, then learn how to become the person who can do those things.

I just can't impress upon you strongly enough that

doing is the only thing that matters. Talking about it isn't doing it. Thinking about it isn't doing it. Asking your friends what they think isn't doing it. Whatever it is, there's no substitute. You can't bargain your way out of action.

Motivation is the worst reason to do anything. If you're waiting to take action until you feel motivated, you'll never get anything done. A professional doesn't care one bit about motivation. They show up and do their job regardless of how motivated they feel. Instead, they let results do the talking. Results will get you motivated, not the other way around.

Chapter 21: What Do You Want?

What does success look like to you? There are as many answers to that question as people on this planet. The fact is, there's no one-size-fits-all answer! I've worked with people who are rich beyond imagination but aren't happy. I've been happy as can be and broke as a skunk.

Success is an intensely personal measure. How you define it is a mix of how much you buy into the standard social narrative, your upbringing, the influence of your friends, your family values, etc. But one thing I know for certain; it's a state of mind. The mind can create a prison out of paradise, or a paradise out of your situation.

Success Logic

Here's a mistake most people make when trying to figure out what success means to them. It seems like a logical approach, but it actually results in faulty conclusions.

Say, for example, that you think Elon Musk is a huge success. You want to emulate his example so you learn everything you can about him. You think, "Since he lived in Canada, and is now a huge success, I have to live in Canada, too!" This is a common mistake in logic that we do all the time whether we're aware of it or not.

You have to build your own success from your own experience, and create your own meaning out of it. The instant you allow someone else to define what your life should look like is the instant you've given up control over your mind. There are as many ways to succeed as there are ideas you can have about what it means. Don't try to imitate anyone else. Be the best version of you that you can be, whatever that looks like. Only then will you be truly unique; nobody else could possibly be you. They don't have the same life experience. They don't have the same thoughts. They didn't have the same family, friends, or lack thereof. You are you, and that's a good thing. The universe needed it, otherwise you wouldn't be here. Learn from others, but live your own example.

Human Excellence

By virtue of being alive right now to read this book, you've won the human lottery. It's better to be alive right now than any other time in human history. You can read! That's an ability a vast majority of humans through history haven't enjoyed. You're already ahead of the curve!

You're also capable of more than you think. Ability tends to find its own level. People with skills tend to go where they're appreciated. Find your tribe. With the advent of the internet, that's easier now than ever too.

My sneaking suspicion is that the secret to happiness isn't doing what you like, but liking what you do, and how you do it. Success is getting what you want, and happiness is liking what you get. Happiness is more an approach than a destination. Happiness is a way, not a place. Happiness is a skill of the mind, just like every single thing we've talked about already!

What a wonderful gift it is to even be alive in the first place. To be dreamt up by the incredible universe for the sole purpose of experiencing all the wonders it has to show us! That is something to be happy about. It's a wild ride, so enjoy it while you can.

Conclusion

There you have it; the culmination of more than 25 years' experience diving into the mysteries of the human mind. I didn't realize it was going to be such a big book! Hopefully I've shown you how to use your imagination, curiosity, interest, and personality to put you on the path to being successful.

If you've gotten anything out of the book, I'd love to hear about it. Please, reach out to me at: jonathan@likeamindreader.com if you feel like you should.

I want to hear from you. Help me understand that this project was a valuable use of my time; I sincerely hope it gave you some benefit.

Best thoughts,

~Jonathan Pritchard

About the Author

As a mentalist Jonathan has appeared on America's Got Talent, entertained United States troops stationed overseas, performed on Vegas main stages, cruise ships, and on down the list goes. Eventually he figured out that the same psychological techniques he uses on stage to make people believe he can read minds, are the same techniques the best companies use in sales, marketing, and every other part of business.

Now, companies like State Farm Insurance, Wells Fargo, General Assembly, Theraband, and Avant Credit hire Jonathan to help them connect with their employees at events, training conferences, and any time people gather; with their clients at tradeshows, customer appreciation events, or hospitality suites; and with their prospective customers through sharpening their marketing efforts. He takes people behind the mental curtain and teaches them how to connect like a mind reader. He loves helping people discover the same magic of connecting with friends everywhere as he has for 25 years.

When he's not on the road he gets his mail in Chicago, practices Wing Chun Kung Fu every morning for the past 7 years, and paints in his free time.

NOTES

Printed in Poland
by Amazon Fulfillment
Poland Sp. z o.o., Wrocław